HOW TO DRAW
CELTIC KNOTWORK

MBC

HOW TO DRAW CELTIC KNOTWORK
A Practical Handbook

ANDY SLOSS

BLANDFORD

A BLANDFORD BOOK

First published in the UK by Blandford
A Cassell Imprint
Cassell plc, Villiers House,
41/47 Strand, London WC2N 5JE

Distributed in the United States by Sterling Publishing Co., Inc.,
387 Park Avenue South, New York, NY 10016-8810

Distributed in Australia by Capricorn Link (Australia) Pty Ltd
2/13 Carrington Road, Castle Hill, NSW 2154

British Library Cataloguing-in-Publication Data
A catalogue entry for this title is available from the British Library

ISBN 0-7137-2492-7

Printed and bound in Great Britain by The Bath Press, Avon

Contents

Introduction

This book is for the novice who wants to be able to draw knotwork in the Celtic style without months of practice. It is hoped that you will be able to doodle Celtic knots within a very short space of time. Those who have studied the traditional methods for several years can do so, but most of us just do not have the time to dedicate to an all-absorbing hobby, so can only dream of such things.

This method is designed to be as basic as possible, while still giving the groundwork of the complexities of knotwork. After all, you only have to draw nine very simple shapes to do all regular knotwork, and once you have grasped these, irregular knotwork is almost as easy. If you can draw the grid, you can draw a knot to fit it. I have tried to keep the instructions as simple as possible, though as has been said 'the simpler an idea the harder it is to describe simply', so if there is a part (or parts) that you can not follow, just try drawing it and you should soon see what it is all about.

This book is not intended to be a manual on how to recreate Celtic manuscript pages, it does not contain reproductions of ancient manuscripts to marvel at and make you wonder why you ever thought that you could do it; there are several very good books for that. It will not tell you the history and development of knotwork and make oblique references to the great Celtic civilisation which lasted two thousand years. It is not even intended to teach you how to draw knotwork the way the Celts did it. This is an all-new, simplified method which I believe is more appropriate to the needs of creators now.

Since the publication of George Bain's book *Celtic Knotwork – the methods of construction*, artists and craft workers have been exhorted to create new designs in this timeless art form. Unfortunately this has led to thousands (maybe millions) of copies of Mr Bain's drawings (often direct reproductions of his original images with his signature removed) and very few new designs. Even those who have pushed the limits a bit, though creating beautiful things, have tended to overlook the most basic rules of knotwork, such as the fact that the lines should go alternately over then under when crossing.

It has been said that knotwork is a visual language, and that once you understand the language you can invent new forms. The 99 sections in this book (pages 64–162) are maybe best seen as the letters of the

7

alphabet of this language, and it is up to you to make up your own words and phrases using them. A word of warning: if you are thinking at any point of cataloguing all the different possible knots, say the border knots up to 5 by 5 sections large, think again. There are 3^{20} or 3,486,784,401 variations of a 5 by 5 border knot so, while it may be a worthy exercise, it would take more than a lifetime unless you use a computer, and the memory required would be absurd.

This method was, in fact, discovered while trying to write just such a program for a computer. It works, but is slow and rapidly becomes pointless for anything other than cataloguing the variations. A revised version, for the user to design their own knots, is now on the market. In this, each of the sections is a letter of the alphabet, so that regular knotwork will be able to be drawn in any program that uses type on any computer. It can then be printed out at any size required, making it possible at last to make knotwork as tiny and intricate as the ancient manuscripts. Irregular or freehand knotwork, however, is still the province of those with paper and pencil.

The discovery of a limited number of sections for all knotwork makes possible much more in terms of craftwork, the obvious being the creation of stencils. Using only about 30 stencil shapes, all regular knotwork can be drawn, thus enabling entire knotwork stencilled walls and floors to be completed.

I hope that this book will help you create perfect knotwork without the limits of a preconceived idea of what the final product should look like. This way knotwork can grow again, full of the life that it illustrates. And it need not stop with what is in this book, which concentrates mostly on the diagonal sections. Once you have played with these for a while, you can always play around with the other two-thirds of the variations – the horizontal and vertical sections. There are some interesting spirals there waiting to be done. Then there are the three-dimensional knots which can be extrapolated from the maths. And so on. Experiment and enjoy.

How to draw Celtic knotwork
(in under an hour)

First, draw a square grid, with half-width squares down each side. At the corner of each square, lines go out either

    horizontally,   vertically   or diagonally.

Where the corners meet, the lines must go in the same direction in all of the squares, so you draw double lines, like so:

So to draw a knot in your grid, draw one of these three shapes over each empty corner like so:

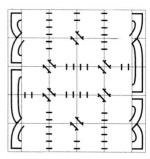

Then join the lines in the top left-hand corner of each square to the lines at the bottom right. Try to draw smooth curves and keep the lines the same distance apart all the way along:

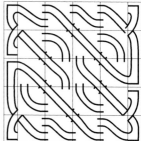

When you have done this for all the squares, join the lines in the top right-hand corner to the lines in the bottom left-hand corner of each square. When your line meets one of the lines that you have already drawn, stop and start drawing from the other line, trying to keep the line smooth. This gives the 'over and under' of interlaced knotwork.

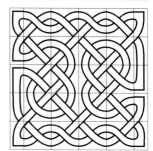

Don't draw these bits.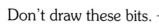

Now you try it, using the same corner pieces as in the example.

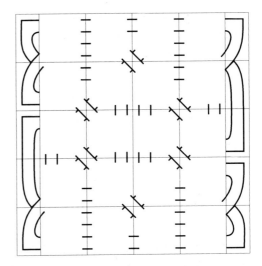

And now draw your very own knot. There are 531,441 possible variations of this shape, so there is a reasonable chance that you have created a knot that no one else has ever seen before, your own unique Celtic knot.

To find out how this method works, read on...

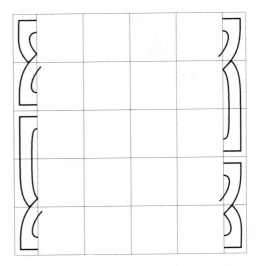

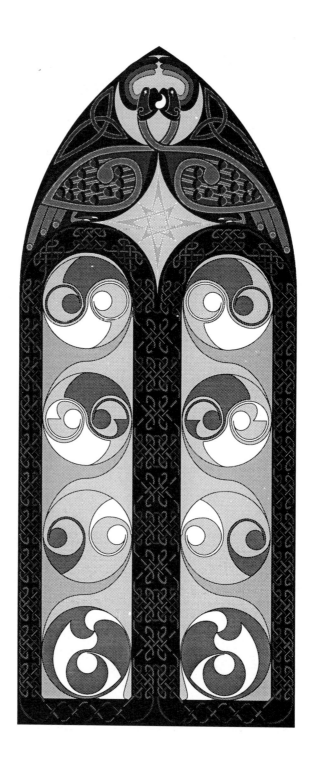

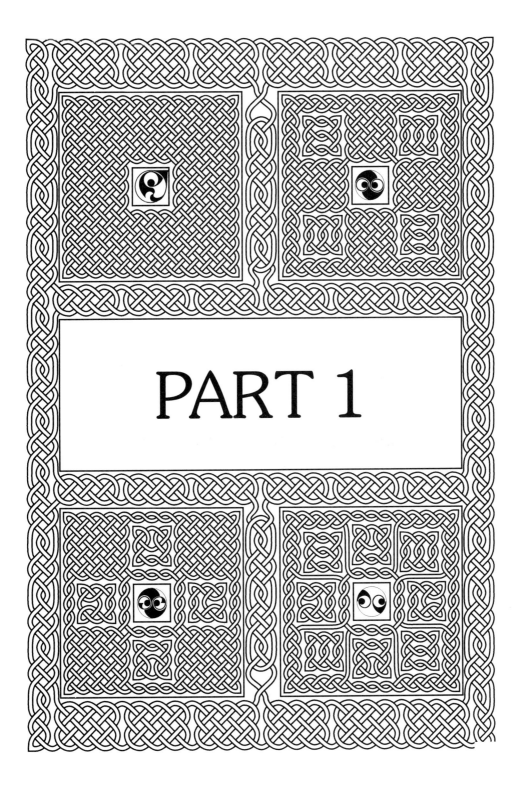

PART 1

The lines

This method was devised in order to draw knotwork using square sections.

On cutting up traditional knots into squares, the lines all tend to leave the squares at roughly the corners.

The lines also tend to leave the sections in roughly one of three directions – diagonally, horizontally or vertically.

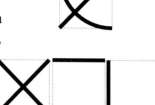

Each corner can join each of the other three corners, creating three more variations:

horizontally,

vertically

or diagonally.

The second line in each section, of course, joins the other two points:

Making this method as simple as possible means limiting the number of shapes that you need to draw to a minimum. Because there are three choices for each of the four corners, the number of variations is 3^5, which is a rather unhelpful 243. Luckily, the diagonal sections are by far the most commonly used, which gets rid of two-thirds of them, so the number of variations becomes 3^4, a much more manageable 81.

But that is not all, because each line can only, in the diagonal sections, join the opposite corner. This means that there are really only 3^2 different lines, and these are the nine simple shapes that you will need to be able to draw almost all Celtic knotwork.

The other two corners are joined by the same nine shapes reflected.

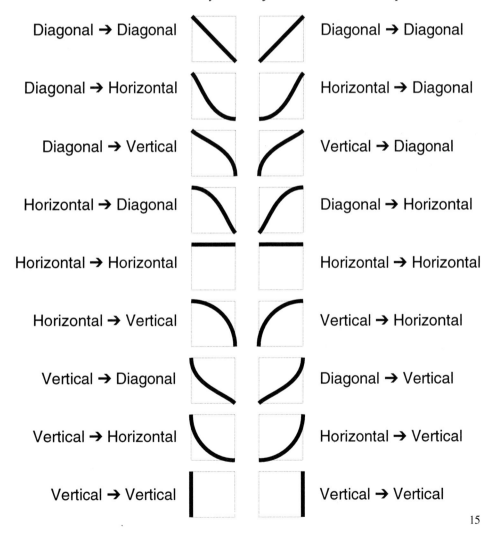

Diagonal → Diagonal   Diagonal → Diagonal

Diagonal → Horizontal   Horizontal → Diagonal

Diagonal → Vertical   Vertical → Diagonal

Horizontal → Diagonal   Diagonal → Horizontal

Horizontal → Horizontal   Horizontal → Horizontal

Horizontal → Vertical   Vertical → Horizontal

Vertical → Diagonal   Diagonal → Vertical

Vertical → Horizontal   Horizontal → Vertical

Vertical → Vertical   Vertical → Vertical

And if you look at these lines you can see that there are only really three different shapes to draw:

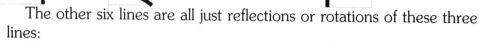

The other six lines are all just reflections or rotations of these three lines:

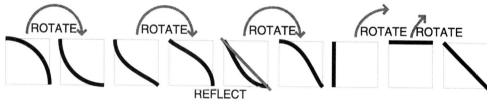

These are for the diagonal sections only. For the horizontal and vertical sections (which are just rotations of each other anyway), these are the nine basic shapes:

As you can see there are only six really different shapes here.

So, believe it or not, almost every possible Celtic knot (and there are an infinite number) can be drawn using only eight different shapes (a straight line is a straight line in all three sets). It's easy when you know how.

Width of the lines

Now the lines shouldn't touch each other (unless they are crossing), so the horizontals and verticals should come away from the corners to stop the lines touching when two sections meet. Also the width of the line in knotwork is important, so we must now move the line from the edge of the section and draw the outer edges of the line, rather than the centre line.   So this...   becomes this.

Generally speaking, in Celtic knotwork the width of the lines is the same as the gap between them.

When you put two together, the gap between the lines in adjacent sections must be the same.

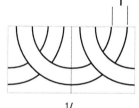

Therefore the lines are $\frac{1}{4}$ of a section wide and $\frac{1}{4}$ of a section apart and $\frac{1}{8}$ of a section from the corner.

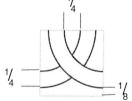

So the eight lines to draw:

become:

17

Square sections

The sections are defined by the direction in which the lines leave the corners:

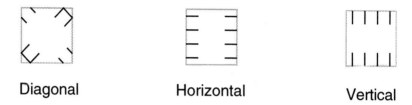

Diagonal   Horizontal   Vertical

and by the way the lines go within the section, though this is not as important because we will almost always be using the diagonal sections, as you will see.

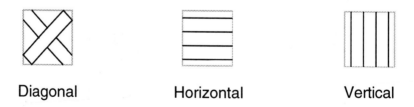

Diagonal   Horizontal   Vertical

Crossovers

As long as you keep the same rules for over and under for all the sections you can't go wrong. In other words, always keep the sections the same way up.

In all these examples the top left to bottom right line is in the foreground (i.e. it is unbroken).

The bottom left to top right line is in the background (i.e. it is broken).

As the foreground line always goes over the other line in the middle of the section, then its diagonals must go under the other line at the corners.

Therefore all diagonals at corners 1 and 4 must be drawn squared off like so:

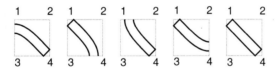

Then when put together the lines cross properly:

No more following the line back from the mistake you have just found to find the mistake that you must have made earlier in order to find out how many crossovers you will have to change that was a common problem with the traditional method.

Drawing knots
The traditional way

The traditional way to draw the knot on the right is, extremely simplified, as follows:

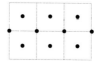

First you start with a grid of dots:

Then you connect them with circles and diagonals to make the guidelines:

Then you rub out the guidelines that you do not want:

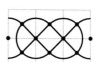

Then you fill in the lines on either side of the guidelines:

Finally you rub out the crossovers, making sure that they alternate between over and under:

The easy way

In this method the central points of the grid are kept:

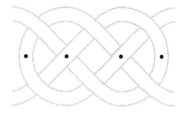

A grid of squares is drawn from them:

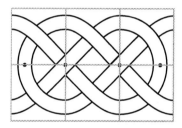

Each of the resulting square sections can be found in the 'Sections' chapter (pages 62–162):

It should be noted that in the diagonal sections it does not matter which line is in the foreground and which is broken and therefore in the background – i.e. whether it is 'left-handed' or 'right-handed' – as long as you make sure that all the sections are the same.

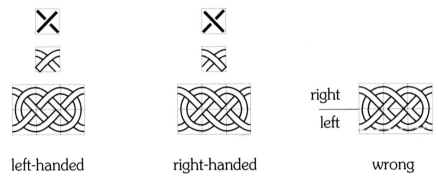

left-handed   right-handed   wrong

So if you reverse the finished knot, for instance when using tracing paper, as long as all the sections are done the same way they will cross properly.

Within the sections, the diagonals need a bit of attention. If the foreground line has either end diagonal, then it must be closed off. This is because it has just crossed over a line (in the centre of the section), so it must go under the line it meets at the corner.

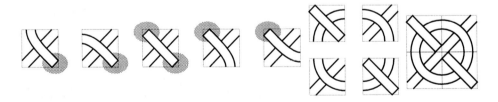

This is of course not necessary for the vertical and horizontal ends as they do not cross each other at the corners. Throughout this book the knots and sections are right-handed, for no particular reason.

The three rules

Using this method, you need to know only three rules:

1. **Where the corners of sections meet, the lines must always go the same way.** Otherwise they do not make complete lines.

These sections meet properly and these do not.

This is also true when drawing repeatable knots for borders etc. The lines down the left-hand edge must be the same as the ones going down the right-hand edge.

This knot, for instance, looks interesting, but when you try to repeat it, you will find that the lines do not join.

By changing the sections down the right-hand edge the knots can be made to join up.

Unfortunately in this example this has turned it into two knots.

By changing the four outlined sections to include a diagonal in the centre, the two parts can be rejoined.

23

2. Top edges of knots must have the top edge lines leaving the sections horizontally, i.e. one of these nine sections.

Otherwise there will be loose lines wandering out of the top of the knot.

2(a). Bottom edges of knots must have the bottom edge lines leaving the sections horizontally, i.e. one of these nine sections.

Otherwise there will be loose lines wandering out of the bottom of the knot.

3. The sections must be drawn consistently throughout a piece of knotwork. It doesn't matter which you draw first, top left to bottom right or top right to bottom left, all the sections in a knot must be drawn the same way.

Smoothing the curves

The one main problem with this method, other than the sheer volume of knots that it can generate, is that as they get larger, the knots get 'boxier'. The 'long curves' lose a lot of their smoothness the longer they get.

The reason for this is simple. As mentioned in the introduction, this method came into existence as a by-product of a computer program which it was hoped would draw lots of things which might look like knotwork and the best looking ones would be used elsewhere. In order to stop it getting too complicated (never having written a program before) I made all the angles as basic as possible – horizontal, vertical and diagonal (or 0°, 90° and 45°).

This could have been done using only straight lines and no curves, but this gives a wickerwork look to the knotwork, and makes it look as though it has been made up of strips of card, folded on the corners, a method sometimes used to teach the basic elements of Celtic knotwork. I was hoping to get something that looked like traditional Celtic knotwork, so I decided to use curved sections.

Using only horizontal, vertical and diagonal angles at the edges of the sections means that the only parts of a circle that you can draw accurately are the semicircle and the quarter circle.

Eighths of a circle use the diagonal–horizontal or the diagonal–vertical lines (see illustration).

Now the distance from the centre of the circle to the diagonal is $\sqrt{2}$ (or 1.414), while the distance from the centre to the horizontal and vertical is $1\frac{3}{4}$ (or 1.75). As the distances are both theoretically exactly the same (both of them being the radius of the circle), something must be done to correct this problem.

And because the correction lies outside the scope of such a basic, rigid system, it must be done freehand, using your own judgement as to when it looks best.

For example, this two-line knot was the logo of a company where I was working when this method began.

Using the sections the knot came out like this: As you can see, both the central top and bottom lines (H – H) and the central edge lines (D – H) are too close in to the centre in comparison to the diagonals. Their straightness also helps to make the eye see it as an octagon rather than a circle.

By pulling out the horizontal points at top and bottom, the circular nature of the knot returned:

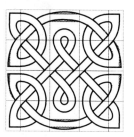

This combination of diagonals with horizontals or verticals should be watched out for when designing knots so that they can be smoothed before the final drawing (or whatever) is completed. Spotting sixteenths of circles, thankfully usually only found in large knots, is harder but well worth doing as this is, to an extent, where the beauty of large pieces of knotwork lies. As with most things, you get better with practice.

One very good way of getting a different perspective on a piece of work is to stop for a break, anything from half an hour to three months, when the basic design stage is complete. Make a cup of tea or coffee, do one of those little chores that you are always putting off, anything as long as you stop thinking about the knot for a while. By taking a step back from the initial design and looking at it afresh, you can often see different aspects of the shape that can be enhanced for the final piece.

Of course you might like the more geometrical, 'squarer' look, in which case keep the sections as they are. No one says that all knotwork has to look one way or another.

If you are using the charted patterns things are simpler because you needn't make any changes. Charting depends on the mind making smooth shapes and pattern out of dots on a square grid.

Horizontal knotwork

First choose the size of knot that you want (for instance, as in this case, 3 x 2) and draw a grid for it:

If you want to make this easy, draw the grid on tracing paper to the same size as one of the grids in the 'Sections' chapter (pages 62–162) – 3 x 3cm, 2 x 2cm, 1 x 1cm or 0.5 x 0.5cm (see Appendix 2). Then you can just trace the sections directly from the pages into the grid. If you want the final picture to be at a different scale, you can always reduce or enlarge the knot or entire piece of artwork on a photocopier.

Otherwise you then mark all the sides of each square at $\frac{1}{8}$, $\frac{3}{8}$, $\frac{5}{8}$ and $\frac{7}{8}$. These are the points at which the horizontal and vertical lines will leave the section. The diagonal ones must be done by eye. The entire grid of minor lines may be drawn, especially when first using this method, to make copying the lines more accurate.

First put into the top left-hand corner of the grid any of the nine sections with both top corners horizontal. This is because we don't want any loose lines (Rule 2). For this one I am using the section which has corners going horizontal, horizontal, vertical, diagonal (or HHVD).

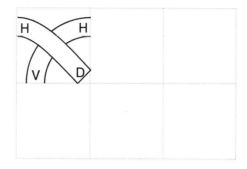

The next section must also be one of the HH sections, but as the bottom right-hand corner of the previous section was diagonal, the bottom left-hand corner of this section must be diagonal too.

So any of the sections starting HHD will fit here.

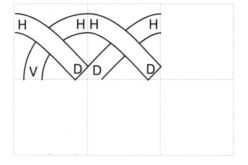

The next section must also be one of the HH sections, but as the bottom right-hand corner of the previous section was diagonal, the bottom left-hand corner of this section must be diagonal too. And as the bottom left-hand corner of the first section was vertical, the bottom right-hand corner of this section must be vertical too.

So this section must be HHDV.

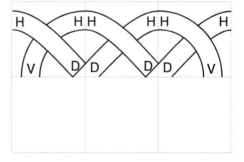

As the bottom left-hand corner of the first section was vertical, the top left-hand corner of this section must be vertical too, and as the bottom right-hand corner of the first section was diagonal, the top right-hand corner of this section must be diagonal too. It must also be one of the bottom HH sections, so only section VDHH will fit here.

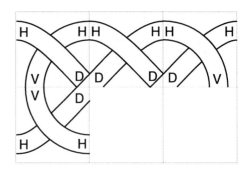

As the bottom left-hand corner of the second section was diagonal, the top left-hand corner of this section must be diagonal too, and as the bottom right-hand corner of the second section was diagonal, the top right-hand corner of this section must be diagonal too. It must also be one of the bottom HH sections, so only the section DDHH will fit here.

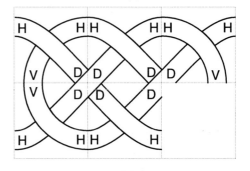

As the bottom left-hand corner of the third section was diagonal, the top left-hand corner of this section must be diagonal too, and as the bottom right-hand corner of the third section was vertical, the top right-hand corner of this section must be vertical too. It must also be one of the bottom HH sections, so only the section DVHH will fit here.

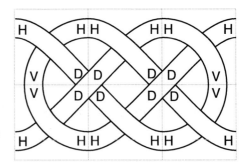

So you can see that the sections can be described by the directions that the lines leave the corners of the grid squares:

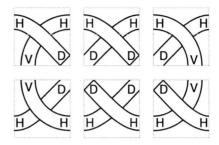

As all the lines go the same way whenever they meet at a corner, this can be put more simply, with only one letter for each corner:

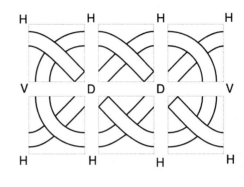

Taking this to extremes, just knowing the directions of the corner points is enough to let you draw this exact knot:

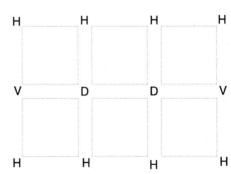

Therefore this knot can be described as the border knot

H H H H
V D D V
H H H H.

Another example

The method is exactly the same for a 3 x 3 knot. For the first section you already know that the two top points are both horizontal as it is the top edge of the knot, and therefore you know which part of the 'Sections' chapter to look in. This limits your choice of sections to one of the nine HH sections.

For the second section you know that the top two are both horizontal and that in this case the bottom left corner is diagonal. Your choice is now limited to one of the three HHD sections.

For the right-hand edge, as the bottom right-hand corner must be the same as the bottom left-hand corner of the first section of that row (so that you can repeat that knot), you know all four points of the section, so you don't have to make any decision at all; the section that you are looking for must be HHVV.

The second row works in exactly the same way: you know two points for the first section, so you have nine sections to choose from. You know three points for the central section, so you have three sections to choose from, and you know all the points for the last section, so you have no choice to make at all.

If you are drawing a knot more than three sections long, all of the sections that are not left or right edges act like the central section in this

example, giving you three choices for each.

There comes the problem occasionally, as with this knot, of the 'enclosed loop'. There is debate as to whether they are allowed in 'proper' knotwork, but they are easy to get rid of if you don't like them.

Just take out one of the sections and replace it with the equivalent section from the horizontal or vertical sections (see Appendix 1). These sections work in exactly the same way, the only difference is that inside the section the lines do not cross. It also connects different lines, thus cutting the knot and rejoining it. The horizontal and vertical sections are, in fact, all made up from two edge sections, so if you are tracing or copying from the 'Sections' diagrams, the edge sections are to be used.

To see how many lines make up the knot, follow one line until it repeats itself. For instance, this knot is made up of one pattern which repeats itself twice, thus making it a two-line border.

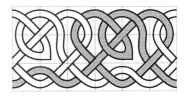

Vertical knotwork

Vertical sections of knotwork must be drawn in a slightly different way so that the left- and right-hand sides can be finished off properly when joining horizontal sections of borders or when drawing knotwork panels.

This is done by connecting the lines that leave the sides to each other. To do this, use the half-width sections on the 'Edges' pages 145–162 in exactly the same way as the other sections. The only difference is that the letters defining them are the two side points rather than the top points.

Thus this tiny panel  would be finished off like this:

This means that when you are designing a knotwork panel and laying out the grid, you must have half-width sections down either side.

So a 5 x 5 grid like the one above only contains 4 x 5 square sections and two lots of 1 x 5 half sections.

The hard way

The exception to this way of doing vertical knotwork is border knotwork. A common use of knotwork is as a border around a page.

There are two ways to do the vertical sections – the hard way and the easy way. First the hard way:

1. In this example the vertical and horizontal knots are the same, though they needn't be and often weren't in the classic manuscripts. When a horizontal knot is rotated to become a vertical knot a half-width section is needed on either side.

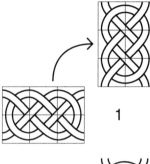

1

2. Note that when you rotate the knot the foreground line of each section swaps over to become the background line (in other words it changes from right-handed to left-handed).

3. In order to deal with both of these, the knot is drawn half a section higher in the grid. The foreground line is now top left to bottom right again, as it is with the horizontal knot.

2   3

4. This also changes the sections required, so the shorthand description of the knot changes too.

4

5. Though it may not look like it at first glance, this is the vertical equivalent of the horizontal knot that we have been using so far.

5

1. First draw your grid, remembering to put the half-width sections along any vertical edge, and put in the knots. Note that the horizontal knot is half a section away from the vertical edge.

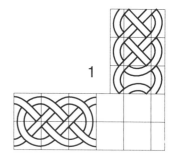

2. From here on in it is just a matter of following the same procedures as before in order to work out which sections to put in the grid.

For the top left-hand blank section you know three of the corners, so you have a choice of three HDV sections.

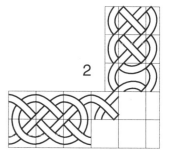

3. You now know all four of the corners for the section below it as both of the bottom corners must be horizontal, so it must be the VDHH section.

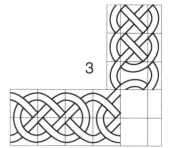

4. You know three of the corners for the next section, so it must be one of the three DDD sections.

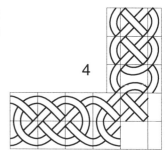

5. There is no choice for the last square section, as it must be the DDHH section.

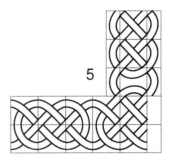

6. There is never any choice with the edge sections – this one must be DD.

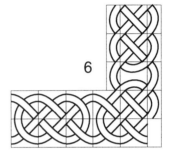

7. And this must be DH.

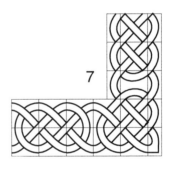

8. Which leaves us with a corner piece that connects the knots. Unfortunately, if you look closely at it you will see that it contains a closed loop. As before, this is simply dealt with by changing any of the sections that the loop passes through into vertical or horizontal sections, thereby connecting different lines.

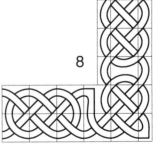

It would be possible, and you may prefer it, to change the bottom square section in the vertical knot into a crossover section. You may like to try this as an exercise, or see if you prefer any of the alternatives – there are quite a few.

The easy way

1. This way works much the same, but you don't need to recreate the knot for the vertical first.

2. In this example the corner directions of the six blank sections has been chosen before drawing any of them, but this is just to show another method – it is up to you which you find easiest.

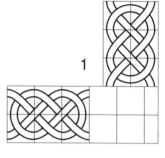

3. We are left with one section that looks to be a problem: the two corners meet one corner between them.

4. In this case, with the single corner being horizontal, the two bottom corners are joined to each other, as if by a horizontal edge section.

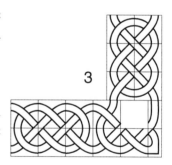

If the single corner was vertical, both of the top corners would be vertical. It could be a crossover, horizontal or vertical section, depending on taste and closed loops.

If the single corner was diagonal, you would have to draw a freehand section connecting the diagonal lines to the bottom corners

The crossover sections:

vertical   diagonal

A bit of a mutant!

Names and numbers

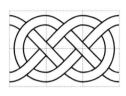

Knot 1

Knot 2

Naming the knots

Using the letters for the corners of the sections means that you can describe each knot individually. For instance knot 1 (above) can be described as the border knot

$$
\begin{array}{cccc}
H & H & H & H \\
V & D & D & V \\
H & H & H & H.
\end{array}
$$

As it is 'closed' top and bottom (i.e. there are no lines going out upwards or downwards) all the points along top and bottom *must* be horizontal. Therefore the top and bottom lines of the description are unnecessary because you know that they must all be 'H', so it can be described as the border knot VDDV.

But because it is a border knot, the left-hand end must join the right-hand end properly when it is repeated in a border. So the left- and right-hand ends of the description must always be the same, so one of them can go. As the sections are listed by their left edge, it makes sense to lose the right-hand letter from the description. So it can now be described as the border knot VDD.

Knot 2 (above), using this shorthand description of knots, would be border knot VDVDHD, but this does not tell us about the vertical section which was used to eliminate the 'closed loop'. It must therefore be described as the border knot $VDVDH^3D$ where ^{3} denotes a vertical section. Horizontal sections would be described by the number ^{2}, and if there is no number, a ^{1} or diagonal section is assumed.

The number is put after the letter that describes the bottom left-hand corner of the section. This is because the top row of points, all horizontal, are left out of the description, and so could not be used to describe a vertical or horizontal section in the first row. This does leave the problem of how to describe a knot that has a vertical or horizontal section in the last row, but there is an easy way around this. For every knot there is another exactly the same but rotated through $180°$, so all you have to do is describe the rotated version and note that it has been rotated. This could simply be done by putting the number as a subscript rather than superscript (i.e. DH_3DVDV, which is not the same as $VDVDH^3D$ rotated).

This still does not tell us its 3 by 3 shape, as it could just as well be a 2 by 4 or a 7 by 2 knot, so the description needs to hold more information. If we know how wide the knot is we can work out how high it is by the number of points given. In order to show the length of each row, a comma should be put in after each row in the description. This way knot 2 is described as the border knot VDV, DH^3D.

To work out the height of a given knot from its description, divide the number of points in the description by the number of points in each row of the description then add 1. In this case there are 6 in the description and 3 in each row, which gives 2; add 1 and the answer is three rows high.

All knotwork that can be drawn using the sections in this book can be described with this method. If you had the patience, the computer and there was a point, you could catalogue all the possible knots this way, from the most boring (H^2) to the most complex.

Counting the knots

If the knots can be catalogued then it must be possible to count them. In fact it is very easy to work out the number of possible knots of any particular size. Of course as knots can be of an infinite size they cannot all be counted and it is not possible to calculate the total number of all possible knots. As the descriptions are all based on threes – diagonal, horizontal or vertical – so is the counting.

There are four corner points to a section with three variations of each, so there are 3^4 or 81 sections. Each of the points can be joined to any of the other points, creating the three different types of section: diagonal, horizontal or vertical. So there are really 3^5 or 243 possible square sections.

When you join on another section there are two points which must be the same as two points on the first section and two new points, both of which have three possibilities. There are, therefore, 3^8 or 6,561 possible matching combinations of two sections.

And for each new section you add, the total possible variations increases by this factor of 3^3 or 27.

When it comes to knotwork borders or panels it is a bit easier. We saw in the previous chapter that for the first section, as the top two corner points must both be horizontal, there are only two variable points, or nine variations on these. Thereafter you know three of the points for all of the sections except the bottom edge (and the right-hand edge in the case of border knots) where you know all four points and there are no possible variations on them.

So the total number of variations of a knot of a particular size is 3 to the power of the number of points needed to describe it multiplied by 3 for the extra possible choices in the first section and multiplied by a further 3 for each of the sections because any or all of the sections can be diagonal, horizontal or vertical.

Put mathematically:

$$x=3^{(ab+a[b-1])}$$

where a is the width of the knot, b is the height, and x is the total number of variations.

This simplifies down to

$$x=3^{2ab-a}.$$

For example, knot 2 at the beginning of this chapter is a 3 x 3 border knot, which needs six letters to describe it, so for a 3 x 3 border knot:

$$x =3^{(18-3)}$$
$$=3^{15}$$
$$=14,348,907.$$

For a 4 x 3 border knot there are 3^{20} or 3,486,784,401 variations; for a 3 x 4 border knot there are 3^{21} or 10,460,353,203 variations; for a 4 x 4 border knot there are 3^{28} or 22,876,792,454,961 variations possible, and so on.

As you can see, the number of variations changes with the orientation of the knot, so a 3 x 4 knot has more variations than a 4 x 3 knot. This is because the points down the right-hand side are not variable in the way that they are in unrepeatable or self-contained knots, which are the same whichever way they are orientated.

These knots have an extra variable section for every row (the right-hand edge) but less square sections, due to the half-width sections down the sides, so the numbers are correspondingly smaller:

for a 4 x 3 knot there are 3^{17} or 129,140,163 variations possible;

for a 3 x 4 knot there are 3^{17} or 129,140,163 variations possible;

for a 4 x 4 knot there are 3^{24} or 282,429,536,481 variations possible;

and so on.

The equation for calculating the number of possible variations of self-contained knots is:

$$x=3^{[a(b-1)+b(a-1)]}$$

where a is the width of the knot, b is the height and x is the total number of variations.

This simplifies down to

$$x=3^{2ab-a-b}$$

So for instance for a 12 by 15 knot:

$$x=3^{180-12-15}$$

$$=3^{153},$$

which is so mind-bogglingly big that I won't even try to work it out.

A sidenote

Throughout this book, the sections are drawn as squares. This is because of the origins of the method and in order to simplify the knotwork as much as possible. In traditional knotwork this is only one of two regular grid shapes.

The other is the 3 by 4 grid and is related to the 3 4 5 triangle of mathematical and mystical fame. The proportions within the sections remain the same.

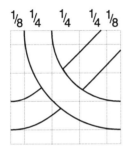

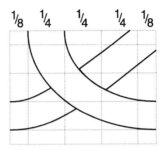

This does mean that the width of the line varies depending on which direction it is going. As a quarter of the long side is longer than a quarter of the short side, a vertical line (A) is wider than a horizontal one (B):

A

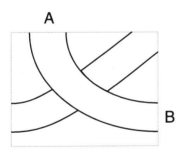

Unevened

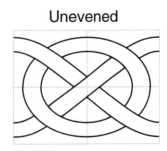

This can be evened out by eye as you go along or when you have finished designing the knot or it can be left as it is with variable line widths, it really doesn't matter; it's up to you. The same holds true for the curves and tapers to follow, as it will whenever one side of a section is longer than another.

Once again, when it comes to the width of the lines in irregular knotwork, it doesn't matter as long as it looks good. And remember – it will always look better to someone else than it does to you.

Freehand/shorthand

All the knotwork in this book can be drawn freehand using the grid as your guide. This is not as difficult as it may seem if you have understood the basics explained so far, the crossovers and the three rules, The easiest way to draw knots is to draw just the parts of the lines that enter or leave the sections, i.e. the diagonal, horizontal or vertical lines. This helps to make sure that you have the crossovers correct at the corners, too.

So first draw your grid – either as squares or, if you are feeling advanced, as the corner points.

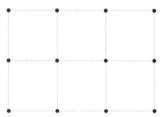

Then draw the lines in the directions that you want them for the whole of the grid.

The diagonals always look like this ✖ , while the horizontals and verticals look like this ＝ and this │ │ │ │ .

Of course along the edges, the horizontals and verticals are single pairs of lines.

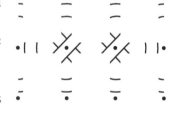

Once you have all these bits of lines drawn, all you have to do is join them up, remembering that in each section the top left to bottom right line is in the foreground, so is drawn first.

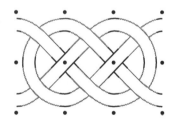

This method is the best that I have found so far for drawing the irregular knotwork that follows, as it gives a very good idea of how the lines will go while leaving plenty of room for freehand embellishments and smoothing.

Example

On the next page there is an example to show you how to design a page from scratch using this method:

First you need to know the size of the overall design – in this case 11 cm by 18 cm.

Draw a box this size.

Mark off the grid with dots at regular intervals for both vertical and horizontal axes. These do not have to be the same, it just makes it easier. In this case the dots are 1 cm apart. **Remember the half-width sections down the edges of the design and each box drawn in it.**

Next draw boxes around any text or similar – any area that you do not want to fill with knotwork. This also applies for any areas that you want to fill with a different pattern or patterns of a different scale as in the traditional 'carpet pages' of the classic manuscripts. Text boxes are treated like the edges, with horizontals along the top and bottom and half sections along the sides.

Go over the whole design, putting the | | | | ‾ and ⅺ shapes over all of the dots except those along the edges. A repeating pattern such as the one in this design (DDVH,DDDD) makes for a more traditional look than a purely random arrangement. **Remember to put horizontal lines along the top and bottom of the design and the text boxes that you have drawn.**

Go through the entire design joining the top left and bottom right lines of each section. (This makes sure that your overs and unders are correct.)

Then join all the top right to bottom left lines of each section (remembering that they go behind the lines that you have already drawn).

Finally join all the unfinished lines down each edge of the design and all boxes, and there you have it.

You are now ready to copy, colour, carve or whatever you want to do with the final piece.

NOV. 1993
£1.50

WET FISH MONTHLY

Non-rectilinear areas
(strange shapes)

'Non-rectilinear areas' just means shapes which do not have straight edges. It also means having to do a fair amount of freehand drawing, albeit of small, simple shapes, so a bit of practice with regular knotwork is advised before trying this section.

The method is just the same as before, with the lines leaving each section at $\frac{1}{8}$, $\frac{3}{8}$, $\frac{5}{8}$ and $\frac{7}{8}$, the only difference is that the edges of the sections are no longer square and as simple as before.

For instance, if you are drawing a knot that has curved edges,

this

becomes this

and these lines

become these.

For instance, if you are drawing a knot that tapers to a point

this

becomes this

and these lines

become these.

Curves

Take a curved area to fill:

Measure the width of the curve and then mark off that length along the side of the curve. These can be adjusted by   e y e , closer or further apart, in order to make them fill the area, leaving a half-width section at each end to complete the knot.

Next, decide how many sections wide you want this knot to be, and draw the grid using the marks to guide you.

In this example the knot is two sections wide.

Then just fill it in with slightly twisted versions of the appropriate sections, following the basic three rules. Note that the 'horizontals' and 'verticals' are no longer horizontal or vertical, but parallel to the edges and grid lines.

Tapering knots

Tapering knots are knots that are used to fill an area that tapers to a point. At their widest end they are always several sections wide, but as they get closer to the point, the number of sections decreases. The best way to do this (in order to avoid drawing lots of lines freehand) is by halving the number of sections each time.

Thus a knot to fill an area that is four sections wide at its widest end would taper like this:

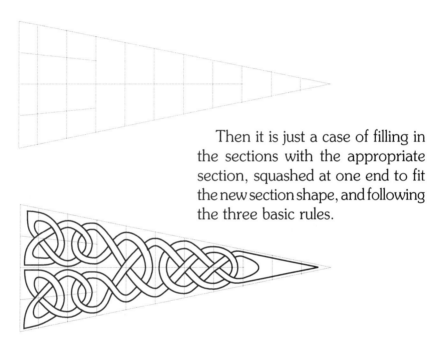

Then it is just a case of filling in the sections with the appropriate section, squashed at one end to fit the new section shape, and following the three basic rules.

As you can see from the example above, the final triangular section, being on both the top and bottom edges, must have both lines entering 'horizontally' in order to remain within the area, so will always look similar to this, while the extra two lines from the next two sections are most easily joined by making them 'vertical', and so leaving no loose ends to deal with. It is possible to use 'diagonal' or 'vertical' lines, as you can see below:

You do not have to reduce the width of the knot by halving the sections, it is just a lot easier that way. You can reduce from 3 to 1 (as below), or by even more, but as you can see, each time you have to do more freehand work, keeping a close eye on the crossovers in order to make sure they go over and under in the right order.

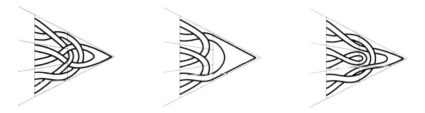

In order to keep the symmetry that is natural to Celtic knotwork, the two extra corners in the 3 to 1 taper should both be the same, or you end up with a lopsided knot:

This should give you an idea of how you can twist knotwork into totally irregular shapes. As mentioned before, just because one style or another is used in the classic Celtic artworks does not mean that they must be slavishly stuck to. Experiment and play with the shapes and you will find patterns that you could not have imagined that are none the less beautiful for their oddity.

Circles

Circles are just a combination of tapering knots and curves, with the consolation that at least all the sections are the same shape.

As with the tapers, there are less sections around the circle as you get closer to the centre, and the smaller the decrease in the number of sections from one ring to the next one down the better, i.e. going from 2 to 1 is relatively easy, while going from 15 to 1 would be a nightmare.

As with curves, the diagonals are not diagonal to the vertical or horizontal axes. Instead they are diagonal to the radial line edge of the grid (the line from the centre to the outside). The verticals are parallel to these lines and the horizontals are parallel to the concentric circles of the grid (the rings that go around the centre).

The only problem is with the centre but, as with the tapers, all that this requires is joining up the lines that enter the central section freehand, in such a way as to make sure that the crossovers continue correctly and that only two lines cross at any one point.

By the time that you get to the centre you should only have two, three or four sections making up the first ring, so there can be 0, 2, 4, 6 or 8 lines across the centre section. In the four-, six- and eight-line versions, care must be taken not to join the directly opposite lines as this would cause a multiple pile-up of lines in the middle.

As mentioned before, the easiest way of drawing a circular knot is to fill in the sections of a repeatable part of the knot and then copy that part, by rotating it around the centre as many times as is necessary to complete the circle. Divisions that are easiest are: 30°, 45°, 60°, 90° and 120°.

This circle has been drawn as a 90° knot rotated three more times to complete the circle, then the central section was finished off like this:

The circle on the previous page illustrates well some of the points to bear in mind when drawing curved or circular knotwork:

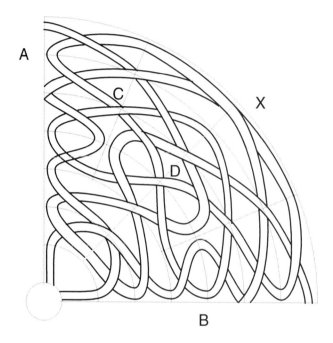

The 90° knot section shows how the lines have been smoothed over several sections. For instance, the line from A to B does not cross the grid at exact right angles at C and D as it theoretically should. It has been drawn as a single line from A to B, making sure that it crossed the grid at C and D but disregarding the angle of crossing, thus giving a smoother feel to the line.

It also shows how you can change the lines within the grids. At point X, both the lines leave their sections at the top edge of the section, rather than one at the top and one at the bottom. This was done in order to keep the symmetry – the section is reflected across the 45° grid line, only the crossovers have been changed. In effect the two sections have been turned into one large one; an HHDD section.

The rules, once you understand them, are there to be broken.

Decorating the knots

All of the sections in this book are drawn like the section on the right. This gives you the outer edges of the knot, and so is ideal for drawing knots where you want to colour the lines and the background. If you want to make it look even smarter, then you can go over the edge lines, after colouring in the lines and the background, with a contrasting colour to make them stand out.

If you want a simple single line, then just ink in the centre line of each wide line, though this would probably be easier if you just draw the single line to start with. All that this requires is, instead of using the grid points at $\frac{1}{8}$, $\frac{3}{8}$, $\frac{5}{8}$ and $\frac{7}{8}$ use the grid points $\frac{1}{4}$ and $\frac{3}{4}$.

$\frac{1}{4}$ —

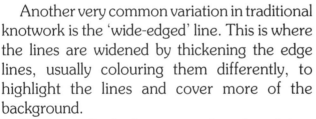

$\frac{1}{2}$

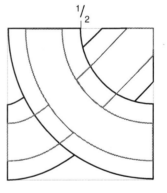

Another very common variation in traditional knotwork is the 'wide-edged' line. This is where the lines are widened by thickening the edge lines, usually colouring them differently, to highlight the lines and cover more of the background.

Traditionally the lines are widened until they touch, which means that each line is half a section wide, or to put it another way, the lines are $\frac{1}{8}$ of a section wide on either side of the basic lines.

Note that the outer lines of the foreground line go over both the inner *and* outer lines of the background line (traditionally, that is).

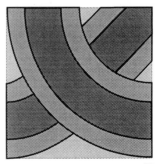

53

Other common traditional knot decorations are shown on this page.

In the first, the outer edge lines are used as the lines themselves. This means having twice as many crossovers, but as long as you follow the rules, there is little difficulty in this. As long as the crossovers in the middle of the section are drawn like these examples, they will always work.

The lines can be drawn any width, depending on the desired effect, using the usual edge lines as the centre lines, and widening them equally on both sides.

The only real difference is that the diagonal corners *all* have a line across them, and attention is needed that they are drawn correctly, or the whole thing rapidly gets out of hand.

Study the third section on this page to see how the diagonals are drawn at the corners. These will be the same for the corresponding corners of all of the sections.

This version is very common, and is simply drawn as normal, then dots put along the edges of all the lines in the knot.

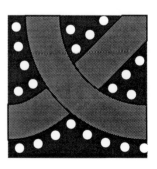

Of course you don't have to stick to the traditional decorations. For instance, here are four variations: rope, 3-D, M 25, and knotwork within knotwork. Your only limit is your imagination.

Where to draw the line
– and how

There are almost as many ways of producing a finished piece of knotwork as there are knots, and with new technologies there seem to be more every day.

The great illuminators of *The Book of Kells*, Lindisfarne and so on used so-called 'primitive' and basic materials – measuring instruments such as dividers, rulers, compasses and styli made from bronze or bone, parchment made of calfskin or sheepskin, soaked, dried, scraped and stretched, pens and quills made from goose feathers, reeds, bronze and bone, and inks made of eggs, fish glue, soot, insects, plants and minerals. The master having designed the page, a fair amount of the final painting and illuminating was then left in the hands of a dedicated team of scribes or 'copiers', the complexity of their part depending on their experience and skill.

The stone masons of the earlier crosses and monoliths used measuring devices such as dividers, rulers, compasses or even parts of their anatomy, markers such as chalk, clay or pointy soft bits of stone and engravers such as small, hard, pointy bits of stone or metal which were hit with a large, hard, blunt bit of stone or metal. All precision stuff for the intricacy of the early knotwork. There is even evidence of the ancient stone carvers using tools for copying sections of repeated patterns in the form of templates. Whether these were made by the carvers themselves or by others is open to speculation.

These days you can recreate the ancient illuminations with modern materials – measuring instruments such as dividers, rulers, compasses and pencils, parchment made of single-ply Bristol Board, waterproof and non-fading paints or inks and plastic or wood and steel pens and artificial squirrel-hair brushes from the local art shop. With a fair amount of study, a lot of dedication and a steady hand you can create illuminations that might still look as good in nine hundred years time as the original manuscripts do now. Of course this will take you an undeniably long time unless you are a professional animator and have your own team of scribes to do all the repetitive and boring bits, but you may well consider it worthwhile to have created a thing of beauty which will last, if not forever, then certainly for a very long time.

At the time of writing the most common method (which requires no study, no dedication and little artistic ability) seems to be to go out and buy a copy of George Bain's book. Look through it until you find a knot (or if you are feeling really creative one of Mr Bain's original and still copyrighted designs) that you like and copy it, either by eye, tracing paper or photocopier. Actually using Mr Bain's methods, though they are almost certainly those of the original illuminators, does not seem to be the preferred option of today's professional. In this 'free market' economy of ours it just isn't profitable to go to all the work of creating something new, when there is a wealth of usable material, easily available, and if the customer has seen the original design before then think of it as advertising for your product. This is mainly true for those outside the graphic arts world – objects with Celtic designs are often copies of Mr Bain's copies.

Nowadays a photocopier is almost indispensable (they are cheaper than the traditional human scribe) at some stage of the process, either to copy parts of the design to be pasted up for the final piece or to make copies of the final picture. A few of the enviable professionals paint their designs by hand and have them printed in full colour.

Of course now there is another way. Using a computer you can draw sections of knotwork, such as one repeatable border knot and one matching corner piece or one repeatable part of a circle and by copying, pasting and rotating them you can quickly and easily produce intricate designs that can be scaled up or down to exactly the size required. The final design can then be printed in as many colours and at whatever resolution you want.

There does, however, seem to be a certain amount of controversy over the use of computers in this field. There are a fair number of craftsmen and women who feel that 'handmade' means making the entire piece by hand. This does not exclude the use of tools such as pencils, rulers, mapping pens, lathes, pyrography tools, airbrushes and even the dreaded photocopier. For them the line is definitely drawn at the computer, the use of which, as a tool, is 'cheating'.

Using a computer as a drawing tool lets you create images of greater intricacy, being scalable, and accuracy, any mistakes being more easily corrected. This is not to deny the charm of a piece that has all the hallmarks of dedication and love, regardless of the flaws in the knotwork or the unevenness of the lines. And just because a knot is drawn on a computer with perfect geometry and perfectly smoooth, even lines, it certainly does not guarantee its beauty.

But it is too late to hide our heads and pretend that if we ignore the advantages of new technologies they will go away and leave us in our blissful, romantic and 'primitive' world. Unless we take advantage of them we will end up as the serfs of the future with the 'druids' of technology ruling our lives with their secret knowledge. We are here to be as creative as we can be, and it is up to us to make the most of the tools available.

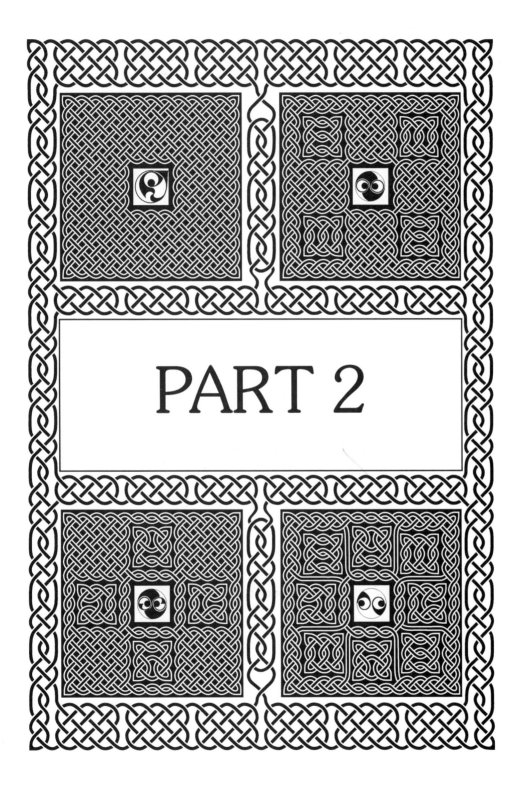

PART 2

Charted patterns

The following pages of sections contain charted versions of the sections for use by the craftworker to create their own designs. Charted patterns are useful for a variety of crafts: knitting, embroidery, counted cross-stitch, needlepoint, crochet, beadwork and latch hook all lend themselves to the use of charted designs. Manuals for each particular craft will explain how to use charted patterns for creating finished pieces. For this reason it is suggested that you know a fair amount about the techniques of using charted patterns in your chosen field before attempting to use these sections or the completed knotwork patterns at the back of the book to create your own designs. These charted sections can also be used for creating bitmap images on TV or computer screens, though there are easier ways of doing this (see advert at the back of the book).

The grids for the sections have been made as small as possible in order to allow as detailed an image as possible to be created. You may find that as you copy each section it is difficult to see what is inside and what outside the line, but as you put the sections together, this should become increasingly obvious as you get a better overview.

One word of warning: it has been suggested elsewhere that to create a large charted design in knotwork, all you have to do is draw half (or even a quarter) of the design and then reflect the portion to complete it – this does not work. Well, it does if you want one side of the design left-handed and the other right-handed, with a line down the middle where the crossovers are all wrong, but it is not 'Celtic' knotwork. In order to make a complete design from half (or a quarter) of it you must rotate the portion as described on page 51.

Traditionally, Celtic art has always used bright primary and secondary colours, and this is what I would suggest; using light colours for the inside of the bands, a medium one for the edges and another, darker colour for the background. This makes the knotwork stand out better. Having said this, it is entirely up to you how you colour your work and experimentation can lead to some stunning novelties.

The sections

The following pages show each of the basic diagonal square, rectangular and edge sections. They are in alphabetical order from HHHH to VVVV. The four basic sections show the square and 4 by 3 line and outline section shapes (as described on page 21), and are in three different sizes for copying or tracing. Each section is marked with grid lines at $\frac{1}{8}$, $\frac{3}{8}$, $\frac{5}{8}$ and $\frac{7}{8}$ so that they can be used for scaling up the sections. This is particularly useful for creating larger stencils for decorating or printing. The horizontal and vertical sections are not shown, but can very easily be made up using the two appropriate edge sections put together.

At the bottom of each page are four charted patterns for each section. These break one of the cardinal rules in that the horizontal and vertical lines come to the edge of the section (except the verticals in the 12 by 9 grid). They also just show the lines, not the outlines, as the scale that they are drawn to makes the sections too small for outlines to be put in, but if you make something with different colours for the band, the edges of the band and the background, it will look as if the edge lines are the outlines. The mind's pattern recognition skills will cover a multitude of sins and smooth out all the curves.

While they are intended to prove very useful to start with, you should find that soon you will not need these section pages as you will either be using the shorthand method or else you will have become so used to the nine basic shapes that this method requires that you don't need to think about them any more. The more you practise the easier it gets.

How to use the sections

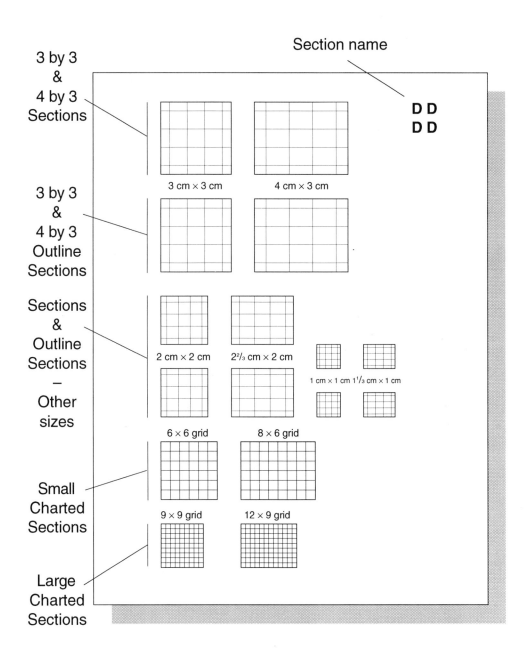

Section name

3 by 3 & 4 by 3 Sections

3 cm × 3 cm   4 cm × 3 cm

D D
D D

3 by 3 & 4 by 3 Outline Sections

Sections & Outline Sections – Other sizes

2 cm × 2 cm   2²/₃ cm × 2 cm

1 cm × 1 cm   1¹/₃ cm × 1 cm

Small Charted Sections

6 × 6 grid   8 × 6 grid

Large Charted Sections

9 × 9 grid   12 × 9 grid

D D
D D

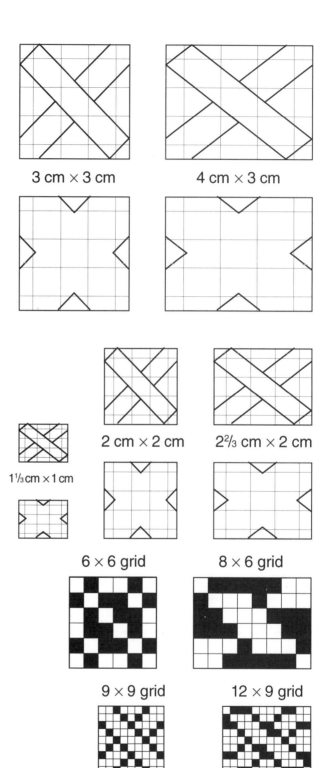

3 cm × 3 cm   4 cm × 3 cm

2 cm × 2 cm   2²/₃ cm × 2 cm

1 cm × 1 cm   1¹/₃ cm × 1 cm

6 × 6 grid   8 × 6 grid

9 × 9 grid   12 × 9 grid

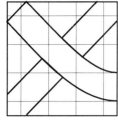
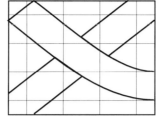

3 cm × 3 cm   4 cm × 3 cm

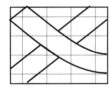

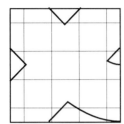

2 cm × 2 cm   2⅔ cm × 2 cm

1 cm × 1 cm   1⅓ cm × 1 cm

6 × 6 grid   8 × 6 grid

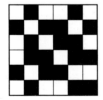
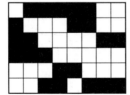

9 × 9 grid   12 × 9 grid

65

D D
D V

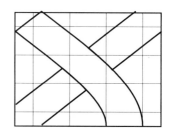

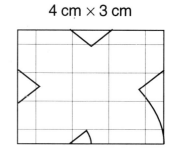

3 cm × 3 cm   4 cm × 3 cm

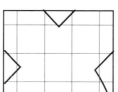

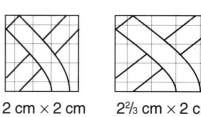

   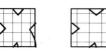   2 cm × 2 cm   2⅔ cm × 2 cm

1 cm × 1 cm   1⅓ cm × 1 cm

             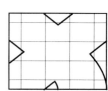

6 × 6 grid   8 × 6 grid

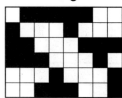

9 × 9 grid   12 × 9 grid

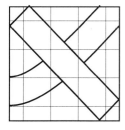 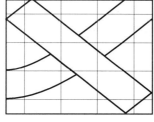

3 cm × 3 cm   4 cm × 3 cm

 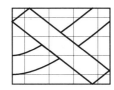

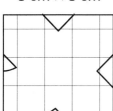 

2 cm × 2 cm   2⅔ cm × 2 cm

1 cm × 1 cm   1⅓ cm × 1 cm

6 × 6 grid   8 × 6 grid

9 × 9 grid   12 × 9 grid

67

D D
H H

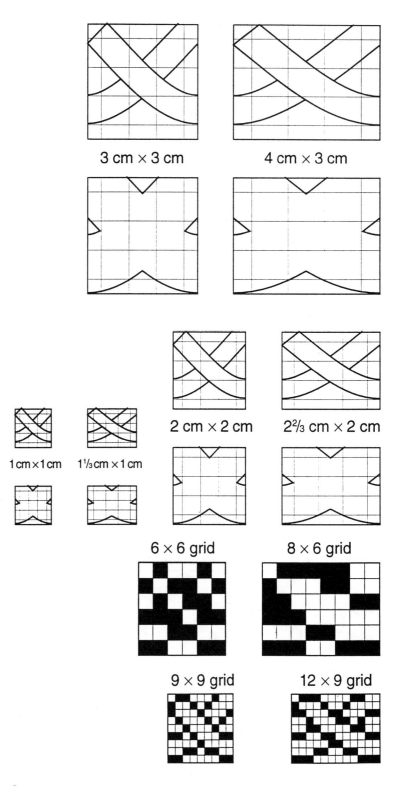

3 cm × 3 cm   4 cm × 3 cm

2 cm × 2 cm   2⅔ cm × 2 cm

1 cm × 1 cm   1⅓ cm × 1 cm

6 × 6 grid   8 × 6 grid

9 × 9 grid   12 × 9 grid

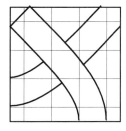 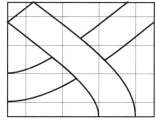

D D
H V

3 cm × 3 cm   4 cm × 3 cm

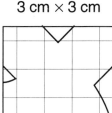

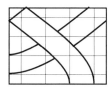 

2 cm × 2 cm   2²/₃ cm × 2 cm

1 cm × 1 cm   1¹/₃ cm × 1 cm

6 × 6 grid   8 × 6 grid

9 × 9 grid   12 × 9 grid

D D
V D

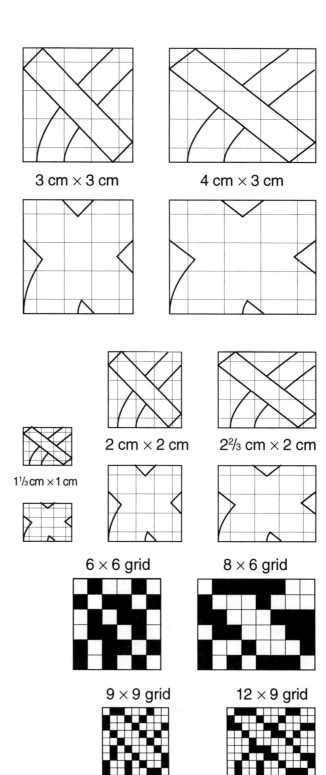

3 cm × 3 cm   4 cm × 3 cm

1 cm × 1 cm   1⅓ cm × 1 cm

2 cm × 2 cm   2⅔ cm × 2 cm

6 × 6 grid   8 × 6 grid

9 × 9 grid   12 × 9 grid

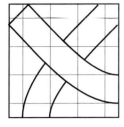

3 cm × 3 cm

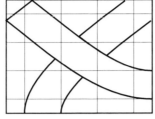

4 cm × 3 cm

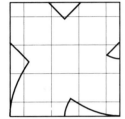

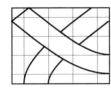

2 cm × 2 cm

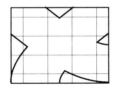

2⅔ cm × 2 cm

1 cm × 1 cm   1⅓ cm × 1 cm

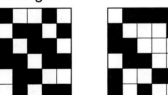

6 × 6 grid   8 × 6 grid

9 × 9 grid   12 × 9 grid

71

D D
V V

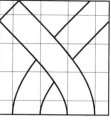 

3 cm × 3 cm   4 cm × 3 cm

 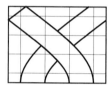

 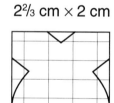

2 cm × 2 cm   2²⁄₃ cm × 2 cm

1 cm × 1 cm   1¹⁄₃ cm × 1 cm

6 × 6 grid   8 × 6 grid

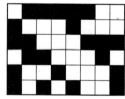

9 × 9 grid   12 × 9 grid

72

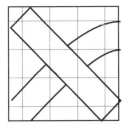

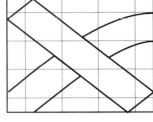

D H
D D

3 cm × 3 cm   4 cm × 3 cm

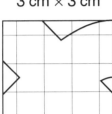

2 cm × 2 cm   2²⁄₃ cm × 2 cm

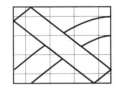

1 cm × 1 cm   1¹⁄₃ cm × 1 cm

6 × 6 grid   8 × 6 grid

9 × 9 grid   12 × 9 grid

73

D H
D H

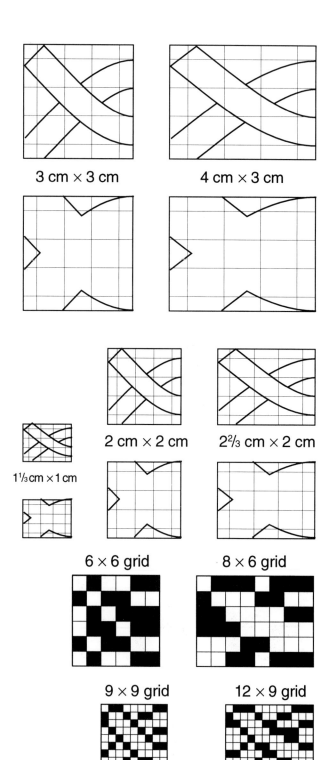

3 cm × 3 cm   4 cm × 3 cm

2 cm × 2 cm   2²/₃ cm × 2 cm

1 cm × 1 cm   1¹/₃ cm × 1 cm

6 × 6 grid   8 × 6 grid

9 × 9 grid   12 × 9 grid

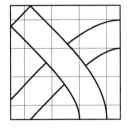 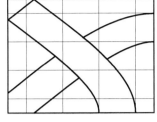 

D H
D V

3 cm × 3 cm   4 cm × 3 cm

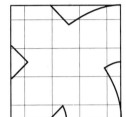 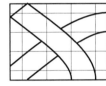   

2 cm × 2 cm   2⅔ cm × 2 cm

1 cm × 1 cm   1⅓ cm × 1 cm

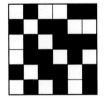

6 × 6 grid   8 × 6 grid

9 × 9 grid   12 × 9 grid

75

D H
H D

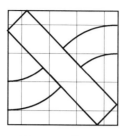

3 cm × 3 cm

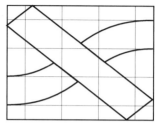

4 cm × 3 cm

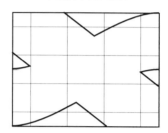

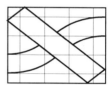

2 cm × 2 cm

2²/₃ cm × 2 cm

1 cm × 1 cm   1¹/₃ cm × 1 cm

6 × 6 grid

8 × 6 grid

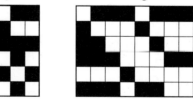

9 × 9 grid

12 × 9 grid

76

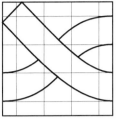
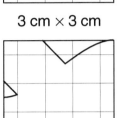

D H
H H

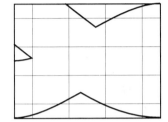

3 cm × 3 cm   4 cm × 3 cm

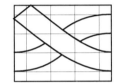

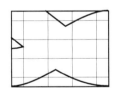

2 cm × 2 cm   2⅔ cm × 2 cm

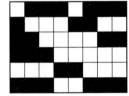

1 cm × 1 cm   1⅓ cm × 1 cm

6 × 6 grid   8 × 6 grid

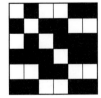
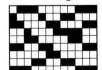

9 × 9 grid   12 × 9 grid

77

D H
H V

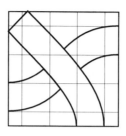 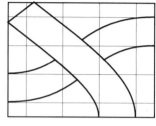

3 cm × 3 cm   4 cm × 3 cm

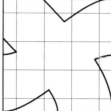 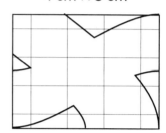

 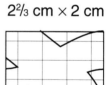

2 cm × 2 cm   2²⁄₃ cm × 2 cm

   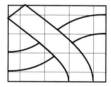

1 cm × 1 cm   1¹⁄₃ cm × 1 cm

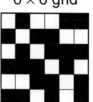 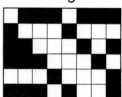

6 × 6 grid   8 × 6 grid

9 × 9 grid   12 × 9 grid

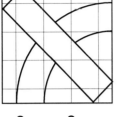 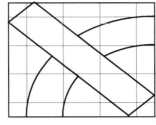

D H
V D

3 cm × 3 cm   4 cm × 3 cm

 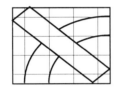

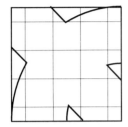 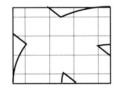

2 cm × 2 cm   2²/₃ cm × 2 cm

1 cm × 1 cm   1¹/₃ cm × 1 cm

6 × 6 grid   8 × 6 grid

9 × 9 grid   12 × 9 grid

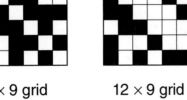

D H
V H

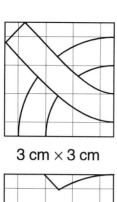

3 cm × 3 cm

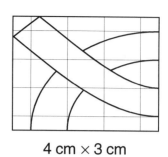

4 cm × 3 cm

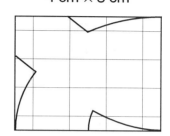

2 cm × 2 cm

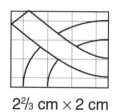

2²⁄₃ cm × 2 cm

1 cm × 1 cm

1¹⁄₃ cm × 1 cm

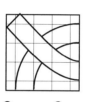

6 × 6 grid

8 × 6 grid

9 × 9 grid

12 × 9 grid

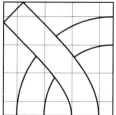 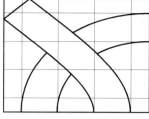

D H
V V

3 cm × 3 cm   4 cm × 3 cm

2 cm × 2 cm   2²⁄₃ cm × 2 cm

 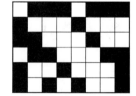

1 cm × 1 cm   1¹⁄₃ cm × 1 cm

6 × 6 grid   8 × 6 grid

9 × 9 grid   12 × 9 grid

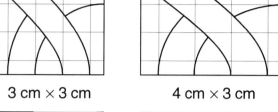

D V
D D

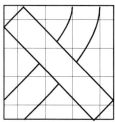 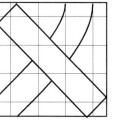

3 cm × 3 cm   4 cm × 3 cm

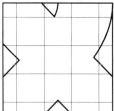 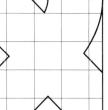

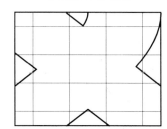

2 cm × 2 cm   2²⁄₃ cm × 2 cm

1 cm × 1 cm   1¹⁄₃ cm × 1 cm

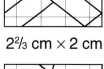 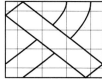

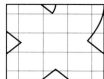

6 × 6 grid   8 × 6 grid

 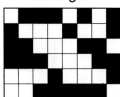

9 × 9 grid   12 × 9 grid

82

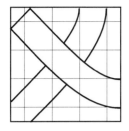
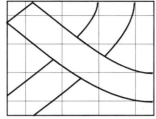

D V
D H

3 cm × 3 cm   4 cm × 3 cm

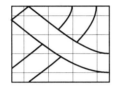

2 cm × 2 cm   2²⁄₃ cm × 2 cm

6 × 6 grid   8 × 6 grid

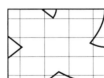

1 cm × 1 cm   1¹⁄₃ cm × 1 cm

9 × 9 grid   12 × 9 grid

83

D V
D V

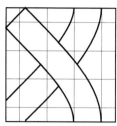

3 cm × 3 cm

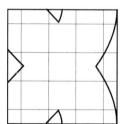

4 cm × 3 cm

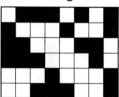

2 cm × 2 cm

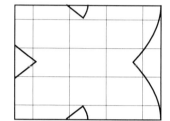

2⅔ cm × 2 cm

1 cm × 1 cm   1⅓ cm × 1 cm

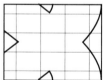

6 × 6 grid

8 × 6 grid

9 × 9 grid

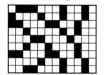

12 × 9 grid

84

D V
H D

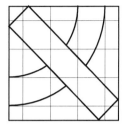 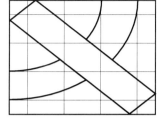

3 cm × 3 cm   4 cm × 3 cm

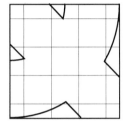

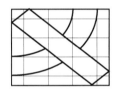

2 cm × 2 cm   2⅔ cm × 2 cm

1 cm × 1 cm   1⅓ cm × 1 cm

6 × 6 grid   8 × 6 grid

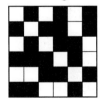 

9 × 9 grid   12 × 9 grid

D V
H H

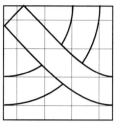
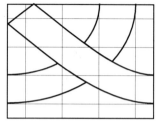

3 cm × 3 cm   4 cm × 3 cm

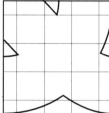
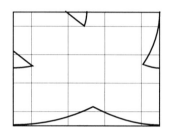

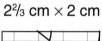

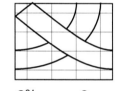

2 cm × 2 cm   2²⁄₃ cm × 2 cm

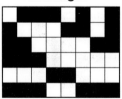

1 cm × 1 cm   1¹⁄₃ cm × 1 cm

6 × 6 grid   8 × 6 grid

9 × 9 grid   12 × 9 grid

86

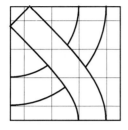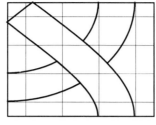

3 cm × 3 cm   4 cm × 3 cm

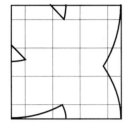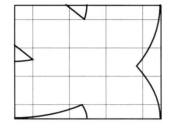

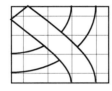

2 cm × 2 cm   2²⁄₃ cm × 2 cm

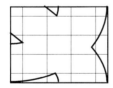

$2\tfrac{2}{3}$ cm × 2 cm

1 cm × 1 cm   1¹⁄₃ cm × 1 cm

6 × 6 grid   8 × 6 grid

9 × 9 grid   12 × 9 grid

D V
V D

3 cm × 3 cm

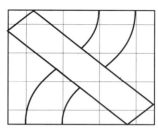

4 cm × 3 cm

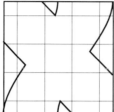

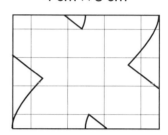

1 cm × 1 cm   1⅓ cm × 1 cm

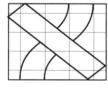

2 cm × 2 cm

2⅔ cm × 2 cm

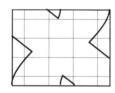

6 × 6 grid

8 × 6 grid

9 × 9 grid

12 × 9 grid

88

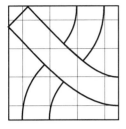

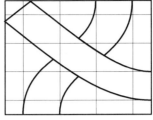

D V
V H

3 cm × 3 cm   4 cm × 3 cm

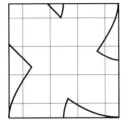

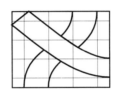

2 cm × 2 cm   2²⁄₃ cm × 2 cm

$2\frac{2}{3}$ cm × 2 cm

1 cm × 1 cm   1¹⁄₃ cm × 1 cm

$1\frac{1}{3}$ cm × 1 cm

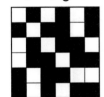

6 × 6 grid   8 × 6 grid

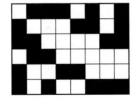

9 × 9 grid   12 × 9 grid

D V
V V

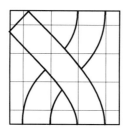
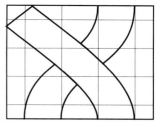

$3 \text{ cm} \times 3 \text{ cm}$ $4 \text{ cm} \times 3 \text{ cm}$

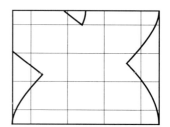

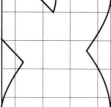

$1 \text{cm} \times 1 \text{cm}$ $1\frac{1}{3} \text{cm} \times 1 \text{cm}$

$2 \text{ cm} \times 2 \text{ cm}$ $2\frac{2}{3} \text{ cm} \times 2 \text{ cm}$

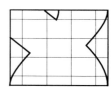

6×6 grid 8×6 grid

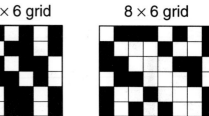

9×9 grid 12×9 grid

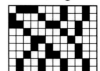

90

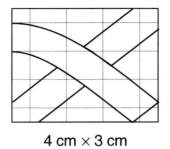

H D
D D

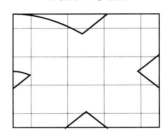

3 cm × 3 cm   4 cm × 3 cm

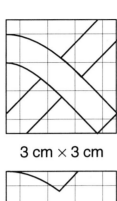
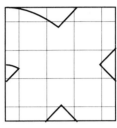

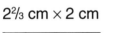
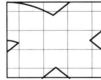

2 cm × 2 cm   2²/₃ cm × 2 cm

2 cm × 2 cm   2$\frac{2}{3}$ cm × 2 cm

1 cm × 1 cm   1$\frac{1}{3}$ cm × 1 cm

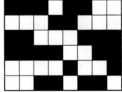

6 × 6 grid   8 × 6 grid

9 × 9 grid   12 × 9 grid

H D
D H

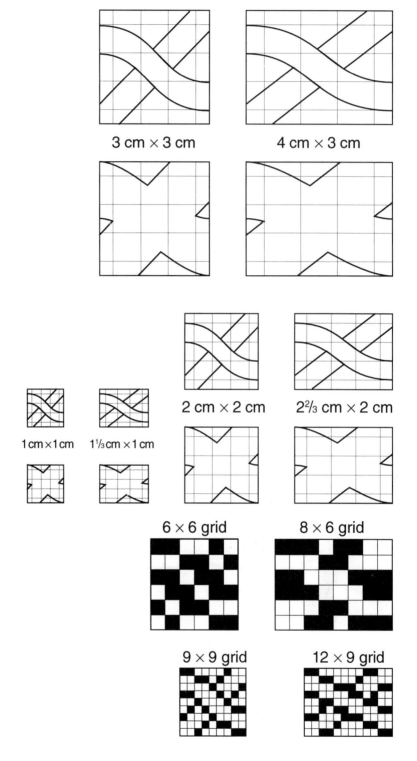

3 cm × 3 cm   4 cm × 3 cm

2 cm × 2 cm   2²/₃ cm × 2 cm

1 cm × 1 cm   1¹/₃ cm × 1 cm

6 × 6 grid   8 × 6 grid

9 × 9 grid   12 × 9 grid

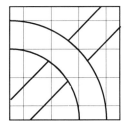 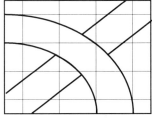

H D
D V

3 cm × 3 cm   4 cm × 3 cm

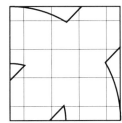 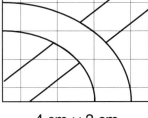

 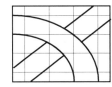

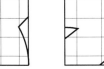 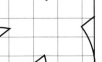

2 cm × 2 cm   2²⁄₃ cm × 2 cm

 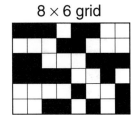   

1 cm × 1 cm   1¹⁄₃ cm × 1 cm

6 × 6 grid   8 × 6 grid

9 × 9 grid   12 × 9 grid

93

H D
H D

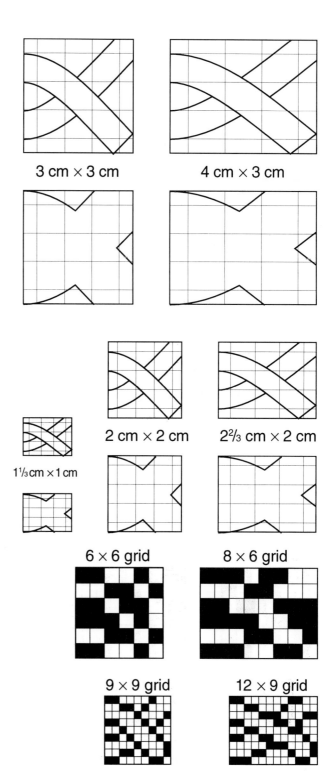

3 cm × 3 cm   4 cm × 3 cm

1 cm × 1 cm   1⅓ cm × 1 cm

2 cm × 2 cm   2⅔ cm × 2 cm

6 × 6 grid   8 × 6 grid

9 × 9 grid   12 × 9 grid

94

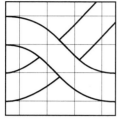
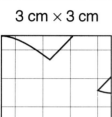

3 cm × 3 cm   4 cm × 3 cm

H D
H H

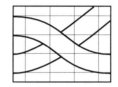

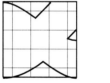

2 cm × 2 cm   2⅔ cm × 2 cm

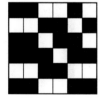
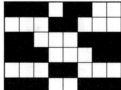
1 cm × 1 cm   1⅓ cm × 1 cm

6 × 6 grid   8 × 6 grid

9 × 9 grid   12 × 9 grid

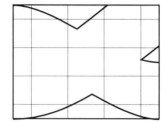

95

H D
H V

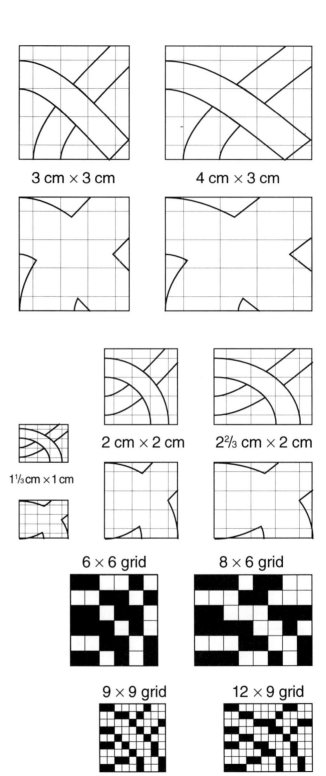

3 cm × 3 cm

4 cm × 3 cm

1 cm × 1 cm

1⅓ cm × 1 cm

2 cm × 2 cm

2⅔ cm × 2 cm

6 × 6 grid

8 × 6 grid

9 × 9 grid

12 × 9 grid

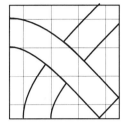
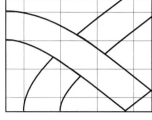

H D
V D

3 cm × 3 cm   4 cm × 3 cm

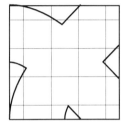

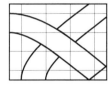

2 cm × 2 cm   2²/₃ cm × 2 cm

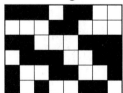

1 cm × 1 cm   1¹/₃ cm × 1 cm

6 × 6 grid   8 × 6 grid

9 × 9 grid   12 × 9 grid

97

H D
V H

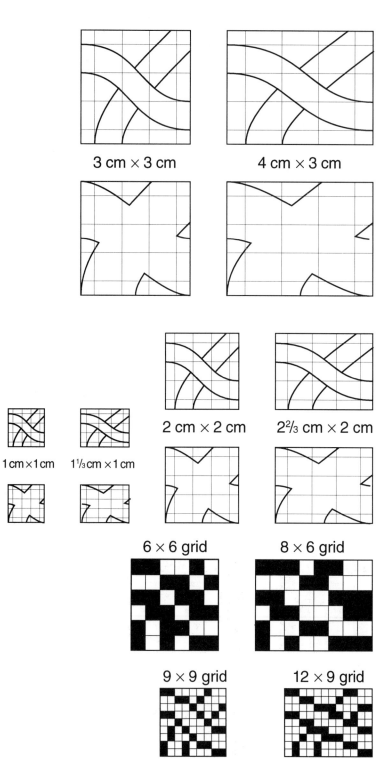

3 cm × 3 cm

4 cm × 3 cm

2 cm × 2 cm

2²/₃ cm × 2 cm

1 cm × 1 cm

1¹/₃ cm × 1 cm

6 × 6 grid

8 × 6 grid

9 × 9 grid

12 × 9 grid

98

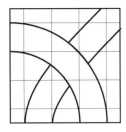 

3 cm × 3 cm   4 cm × 3 cm

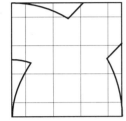 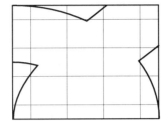

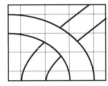

2 cm × 2 cm   2²/₃ cm × 2 cm

1 cm × 1 cm   1¹/₃ cm × 1 cm

6 × 6 grid   8 × 6 grid

9 × 9 grid   12 × 9 grid

H H
D D

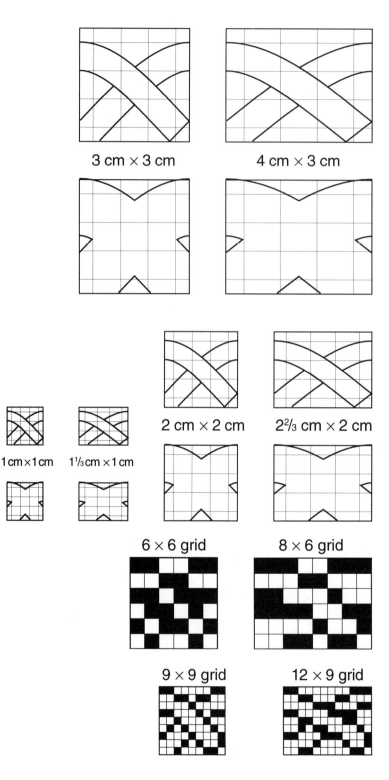

3 cm × 3 cm   4 cm × 3 cm

2 cm × 2 cm   2⅔ cm × 2 cm

1 cm × 1 cm   1⅓ cm × 1 cm

6 × 6 grid   8 × 6 grid

9 × 9 grid   12 × 9 grid

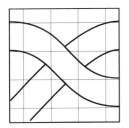
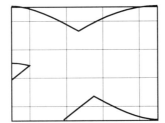

H H
D H

3 cm × 3 cm   4 cm × 3 cm

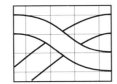

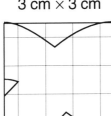

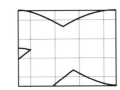

2 cm × 2 cm   2⅔ cm × 2 cm

1 cm × 1 cm   1⅓ cm × 1 cm

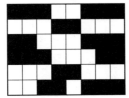

6 × 6 grid   8 × 6 grid

9 × 9 grid   12 × 9 grid

H H
D V

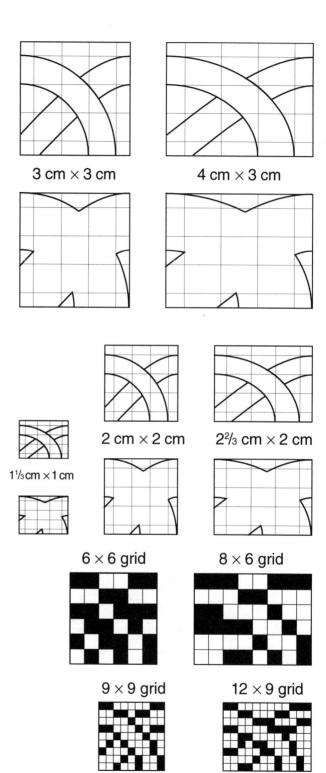

3 cm × 3 cm

4 cm × 3 cm

2 cm × 2 cm

2⅔ cm × 2 cm

1 cm × 1 cm

1⅓ cm × 1 cm

6 × 6 grid

8 × 6 grid

9 × 9 grid

12 × 9 grid

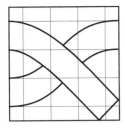 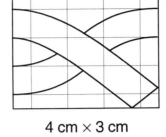

H H
H D

3 cm × 3 cm   4 cm × 3 cm

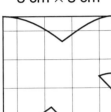

 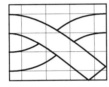

2 cm × 2 cm   2²⁄₃ cm × 2 cm

1 cm × 1 cm   1¹⁄₃ cm × 1 cm

6 × 6 grid   8 × 6 grid

9 × 9 grid   12 × 9 grid

H H
H H

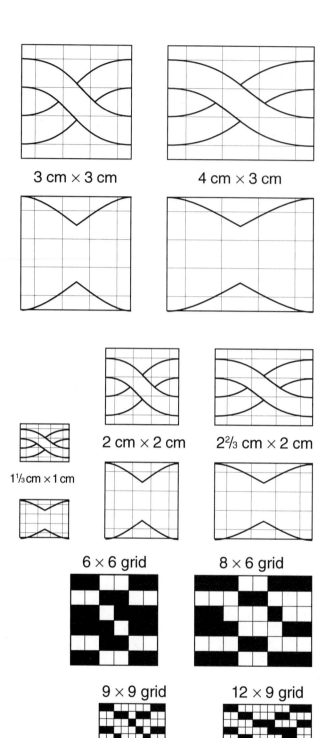

3 cm × 3 cm   4 cm × 3 cm

2 cm × 2 cm   2²⁄₃ cm × 2 cm

1 cm × 1 cm   1¹⁄₃ cm × 1 cm

6 × 6 grid   8 × 6 grid

9 × 9 grid   12 × 9 grid

104

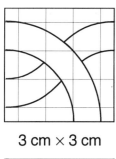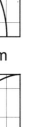

H H
H V

3 cm × 3 cm   4 cm × 3 cm

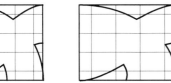

2 cm × 2 cm   2²⁄₃ cm × 2 cm

1 cm × 1 cm   1¹⁄₃ cm × 1 cm

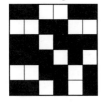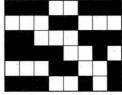

6 × 6 grid   8 × 6 grid

9 × 9 grid   12 × 9 grid

H H
V D

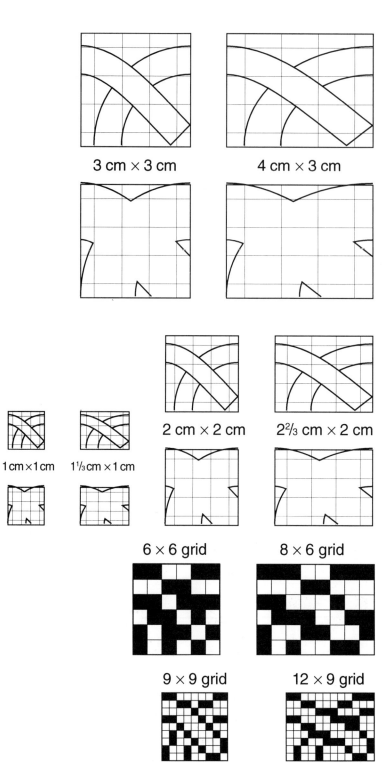

3 cm × 3 cm   4 cm × 3 cm

2 cm × 2 cm   2²/₃ cm × 2 cm

1 cm × 1 cm   1¹/₃ cm × 1 cm

6 × 6 grid   8 × 6 grid

9 × 9 grid   12 × 9 grid

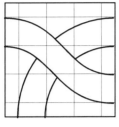
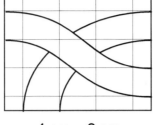

H H
V H

3 cm × 3 cm   4 cm × 3 cm

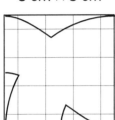

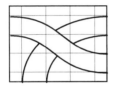

2 cm × 2 cm   2²⁄₃ cm × 2 cm

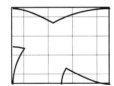

1 cm × 1 cm   1¹⁄₃ cm × 1 cm

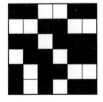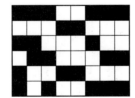

6 × 6 grid   8 × 6 grid

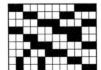

9 × 9 grid   12 × 9 grid

107

H H
V V

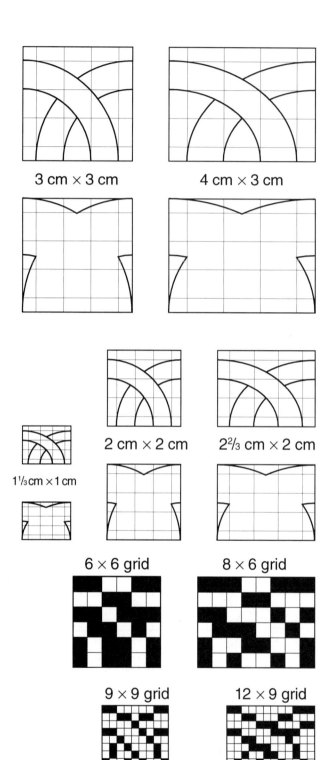

3 cm × 3 cm   4 cm × 3 cm

2 cm × 2 cm   2⅔ cm × 2 cm

1 cm × 1 cm   1⅓ cm × 1 cm

6 × 6 grid   8 × 6 grid

9 × 9 grid   12 × 9 grid

108

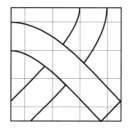 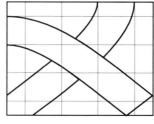

3 cm × 3 cm   4 cm × 3 cm

H V
D D

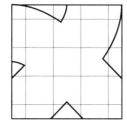 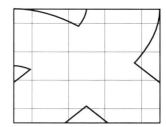

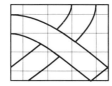

2 cm × 2 cm   2²⁄₃ cm × 2 cm

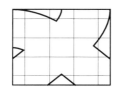

1 cm × 1 cm   1¹⁄₃ cm × 1 cm

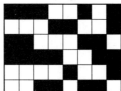

6 × 6 grid   8 × 6 grid

9 × 9 grid   12 × 9 grid

109

H V
D H

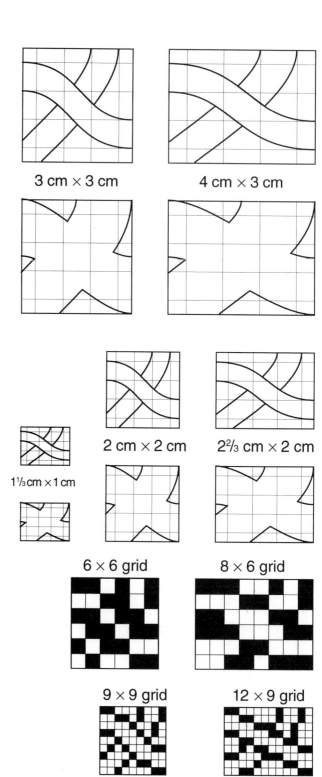

3 cm × 3 cm

4 cm × 3 cm

2 cm × 2 cm

2²⁄₃ cm × 2 cm

1 cm × 1 cm

1¹⁄₃ cm × 1 cm

6 × 6 grid

8 × 6 grid

9 × 9 grid

12 × 9 grid

110

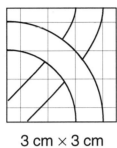 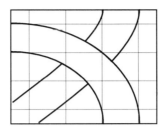

H V
D V

3 cm × 3 cm   4 cm × 3 cm

 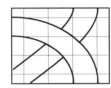

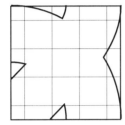

2 cm × 2 cm   2²⁄₃ cm × 2 cm

1 cm × 1 cm   1¹⁄₃ cm × 1 cm

 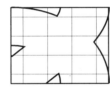

6 × 6 grid   8 × 6 grid

9 × 9 grid   12 × 9 grid

111

H V
H D

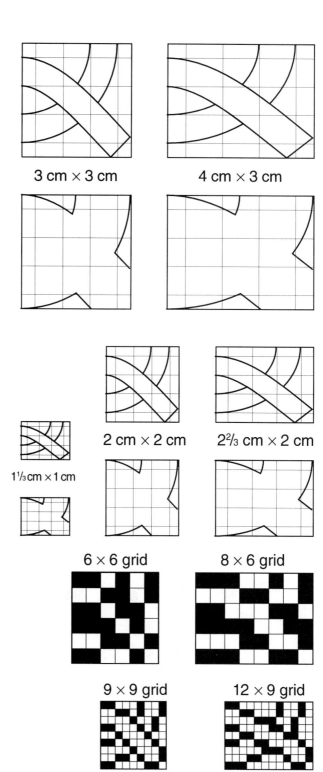

3 cm × 3 cm

4 cm × 3 cm

1 cm × 1 cm

1⅓ cm × 1 cm

2 cm × 2 cm

2⅔ cm × 2 cm

6 × 6 grid

8 × 6 grid

9 × 9 grid

12 × 9 grid

112

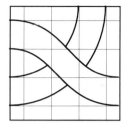 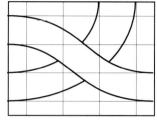

H V
H H

3 cm × 3 cm　　　　4 cm × 3 cm

 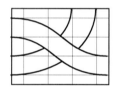

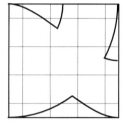 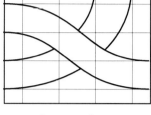

2 cm × 2 cm　　2⅔ cm × 2 cm

1 cm × 1 cm　　1⅓ cm × 1 cm

6 × 6 grid　　　　8 × 6 grid

9 × 9 grid　　　12 × 9 grid

113

H V
H V

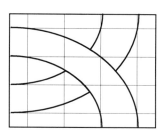

3 cm × 3 cm

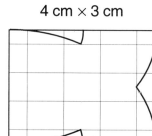

4 cm × 3 cm

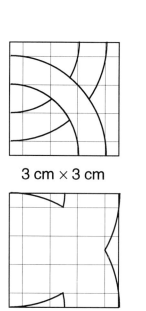

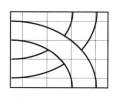

2 cm × 2 cm

2²⁄₃ cm × 2 cm

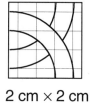

1 cm × 1 cm   1¹⁄₃ cm × 1 cm

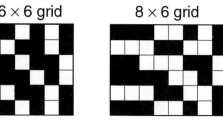

6 × 6 grid

8 × 6 grid

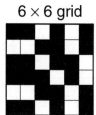

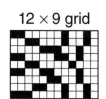

9 × 9 grid

12 × 9 grid

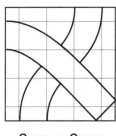

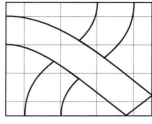

H V
V D

3 cm × 3 cm   4 cm × 3 cm

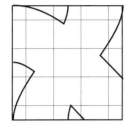

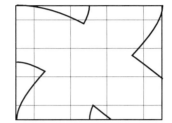

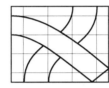

2 cm × 2 cm   2⅔ cm × 2 cm

1 cm × 1 cm   1⅓ cm × 1 cm

6 × 6 grid   8 × 6 grid

9 × 9 grid   12 × 9 grid

115

H V
V H

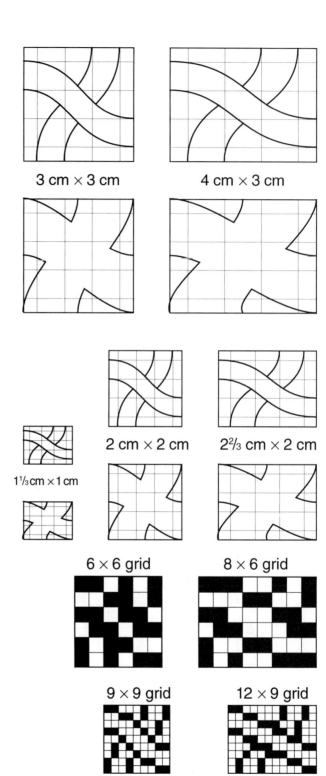

3 cm × 3 cm   4 cm × 3 cm

2 cm × 2 cm   2²⁄₃ cm × 2 cm

1 cm × 1 cm   1¹⁄₃ cm × 1 cm

6 × 6 grid   8 × 6 grid

9 × 9 grid   12 × 9 grid

116

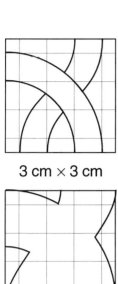

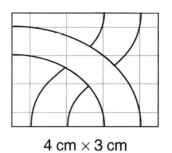

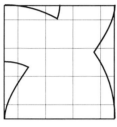

H V
V V

3 cm × 3 cm   4 cm × 3 cm

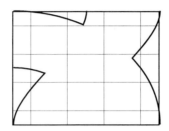

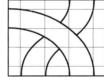

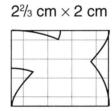

2 cm × 2 cm   2²⁄₃ cm × 2 cm

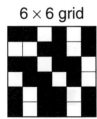

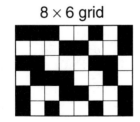

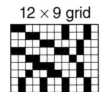

1 cm × 1 cm   1¹⁄₃ cm × 1 cm

6 × 6 grid   8 × 6 grid

9 × 9 grid   12 × 9 grid

V D
D D

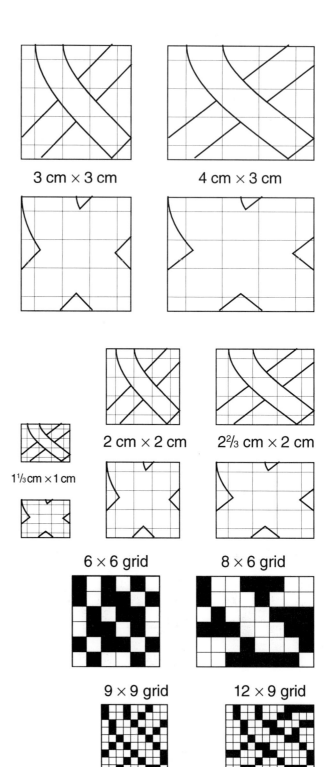

3 cm × 3 cm   4 cm × 3 cm

1 cm × 1 cm   1⅓ cm × 1 cm   2 cm × 2 cm   2⅔ cm × 2 cm

6 × 6 grid   8 × 6 grid

9 × 9 grid   12 × 9 grid

118

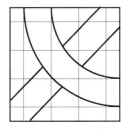

V D
D H

3 cm × 3 cm   4 cm × 3 cm

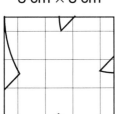

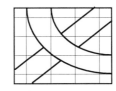

2 cm × 2 cm   2²⁄₃ cm × 2 cm

1 cm × 1 cm   1¹⁄₃ cm × 1 cm

          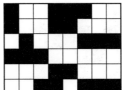

6 × 6 grid   8 × 6 grid

9 × 9 grid   12 × 9 grid

119

V D
D V

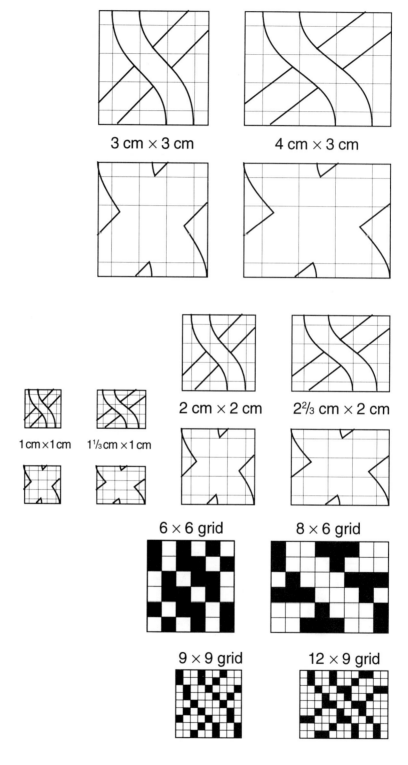

3 cm × 3 cm   4 cm × 3 cm

2 cm × 2 cm   2²/₃ cm × 2 cm

1 cm × 1 cm   1¹/₃ cm × 1 cm

6 × 6 grid   8 × 6 grid

9 × 9 grid   12 × 9 grid

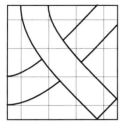

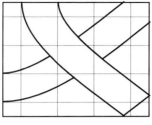

V D
H D

3 cm × 3 cm   4 cm × 3 cm

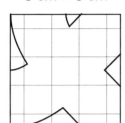

2 cm × 2 cm   2²/₃ cm × 2 cm

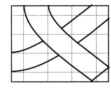

1 cm × 1 cm   1¹/₃ cm × 1 cm

6 × 6 grid   8 × 6 grid

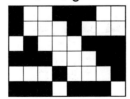

9 × 9 grid   12 × 9 grid

121

V D
H H

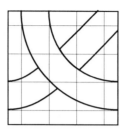
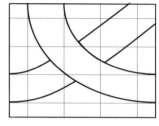

3 cm × 3 cm   4 cm × 3 cm

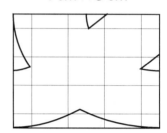

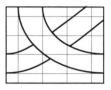

2 cm × 2 cm   2²⁄₃ cm × 2 cm

1 cm × 1 cm   1¹⁄₃ cm × 1 cm

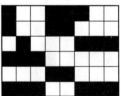

6 × 6 grid   8 × 6 grid

9 × 9 grid   12 × 9 grid

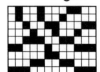

122

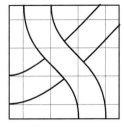 

V D
H V

3 cm × 3 cm   4 cm × 3 cm

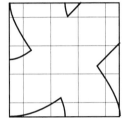 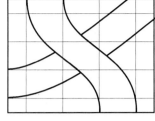

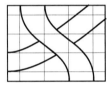 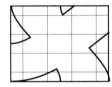

2 cm × 2 cm   2⅔ cm × 2 cm

1 cm × 1 cm   1⅓ cm × 1 cm

6 × 6 grid   8 × 6 grid

9 × 9 grid   12 × 9 grid

V D
V D

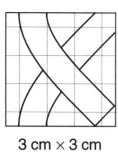
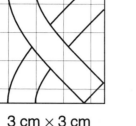

3 cm × 3 cm   4 cm × 3 cm

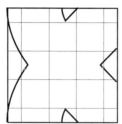
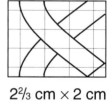

2 cm × 2 cm   2²⁄₃ cm × 2 cm

1 cm × 1 cm   1¹⁄₃ cm × 1 cm

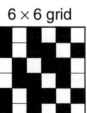

6 × 6 grid   8 × 6 grid

9 × 9 grid   12 × 9 grid

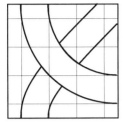 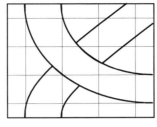

V D
V H

3 cm × 3 cm   4 cm × 3 cm

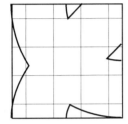 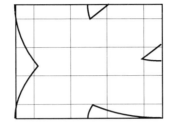

 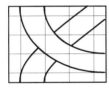

2 cm × 2 cm   2²/₃ cm × 2 cm

1 cm × 1 cm   1¹/₃ cm × 1 cm

 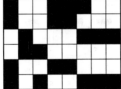

6 × 6 grid   8 × 6 grid

9 × 9 grid   12 × 9 grid

125

V D
V V

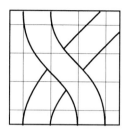
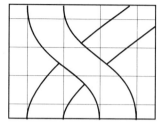

3 cm × 3 cm   4 cm × 3 cm

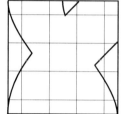
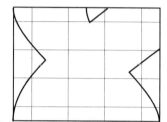

2 cm × 2 cm   2²⁄₃ cm × 2 cm

1 cm × 1 cm   1¹⁄₃ cm × 1 cm

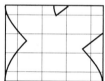

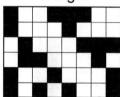

6 × 6 grid   8 × 6 grid

9 × 9 grid   12 × 9 grid

126

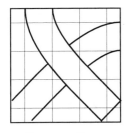

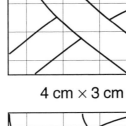

3 cm × 3 cm   4 cm × 3 cm

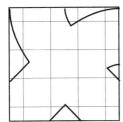

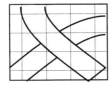

2 cm × 2 cm   2²⁄₃ cm × 2 cm

1 cm × 1 cm   1¹⁄₃ cm × 1 cm

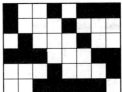

6 × 6 grid   8 × 6 grid

9 × 9 grid   12 × 9 grid

127

V H
D H

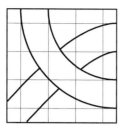

3 cm × 3 cm

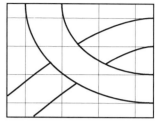

4 cm × 3 cm

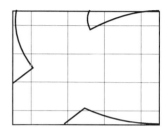

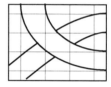

2 cm × 2 cm

2²⁄₃ cm × 2 cm

1 cm × 1 cm   1¹⁄₃ cm × 1 cm

6 × 6 grid

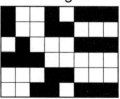

8 × 6 grid

9 × 9 grid

12 × 9 grid

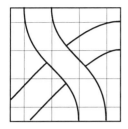 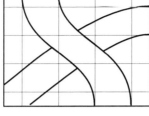

$$\begin{array}{c} \textbf{V H} \\ \textbf{D V} \end{array}$$

3 cm × 3 cm   4 cm × 3 cm

 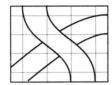

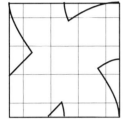 

2 cm × 2 cm   2⅔ cm × 2 cm

1 cm × 1 cm   1⅓ cm × 1 cm

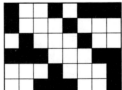

6 × 6 grid   8 × 6 grid

9 × 9 grid   12 × 9 grid

V H
H D

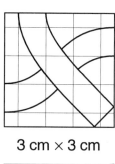
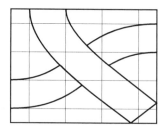

3 cm × 3 cm   4 cm × 3 cm

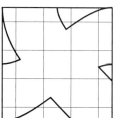
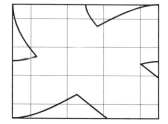

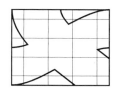

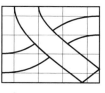

2 cm × 2 cm   2²⁄₃ cm × 2 cm

1 cm × 1 cm   1¹⁄₃ cm × 1 cm

6 × 6 grid   8 × 6 grid

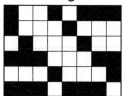

9 × 9 grid   12 × 9 grid

130

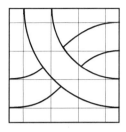 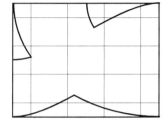

V H
H H

3 cm × 3 cm   4 cm × 3 cm

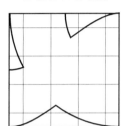 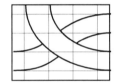

2 cm × 2 cm   2⅔ cm × 2 cm

 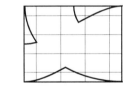

1 cm × 1 cm   1⅓ cm × 1 cm

 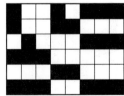

6 × 6 grid   8 × 6 grid

9 × 9 grid   12 × 9 grid

131

V H
H V

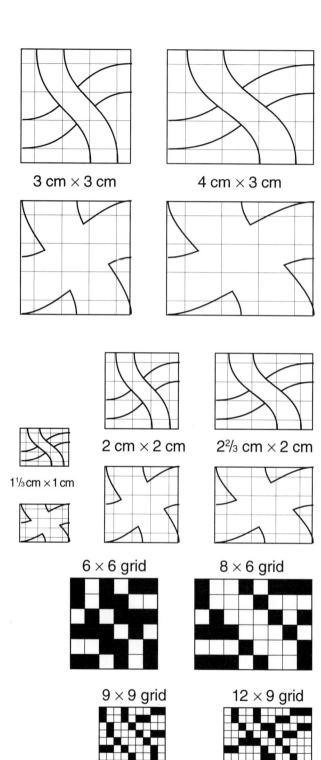

3 cm × 3 cm   4 cm × 3 cm

2 cm × 2 cm   2²/₃ cm × 2 cm

1 cm × 1 cm   1¹/₃ cm × 1 cm

6 × 6 grid   8 × 6 grid

9 × 9 grid   12 × 9 grid

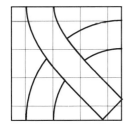 

V H
V D

3 cm × 3 cm   4 cm × 3 cm

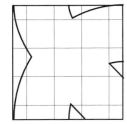 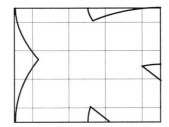

2 cm × 2 cm   2²/₃ cm × 2 cm

 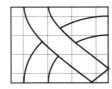

1 cm × 1 cm   1¹/₃ cm × 1 cm

 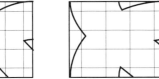

6 × 6 grid   8 × 6 grid

  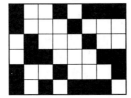

9 × 9 grid   12 × 9 grid

V H
V H

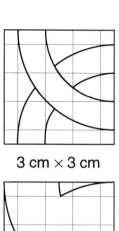
3 cm × 3 cm

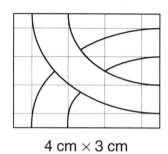
4 cm × 3 cm

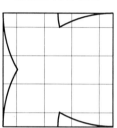

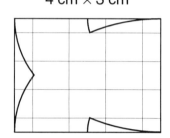

2 cm × 2 cm

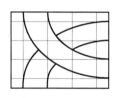
2²/₃ cm × 2 cm

1 cm × 1 cm

1¹/₃ cm × 1 cm

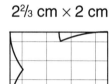

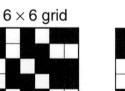
6 × 6 grid

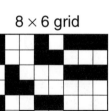
8 × 6 grid

9 × 9 grid

12 × 9 grid

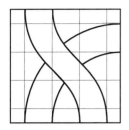 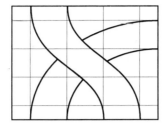

V H
V V

3 cm × 3 cm   4 cm × 3 cm

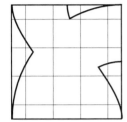 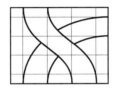

2 cm × 2 cm   2²⁄₃ cm × 2 cm

1 cm × 1 cm   1¹⁄₃ cm × 1 cm

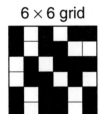 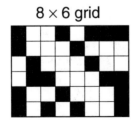

6 × 6 grid   8 × 6 grid

9 × 9 grid   12 × 9 grid

135

V V
D D

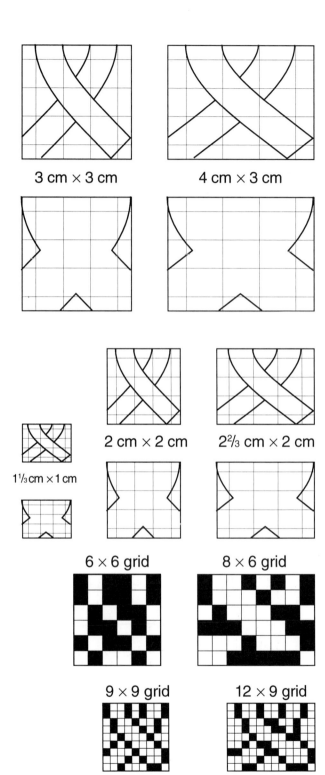

3 cm × 3 cm   4 cm × 3 cm

1 cm × 1 cm   1⅓ cm × 1 cm

2 cm × 2 cm   2⅔ cm × 2 cm

6 × 6 grid   8 × 6 grid

9 × 9 grid   12 × 9 grid

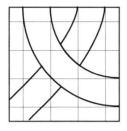 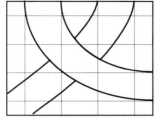

V V
D H

3 cm × 3 cm   4 cm × 3 cm

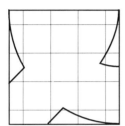

 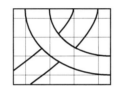

2 cm × 2 cm   2⅔ cm × 2 cm

 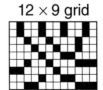

1 cm × 1 cm   1⅓ cm × 1 cm

 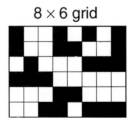

6 × 6 grid   8 × 6 grid

9 × 9 grid   12 × 9 grid

137

V V
D V

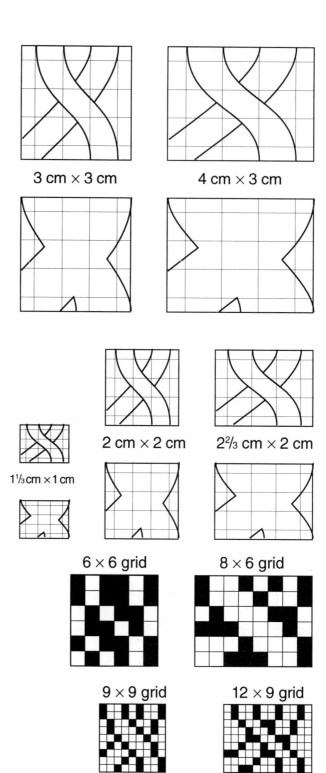

3 cm × 3 cm   4 cm × 3 cm

2 cm × 2 cm   2⅔ cm × 2 cm

1 cm × 1 cm   1⅓ cm × 1 cm

6 × 6 grid   8 × 6 grid

9 × 9 grid   12 × 9 grid

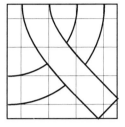 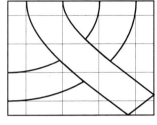 **V V**
H D

3 cm × 3 cm   4 cm × 3 cm

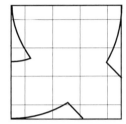

 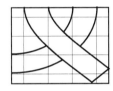

2 cm × 2 cm   2²/₃ cm × 2 cm

1 cm × 1 cm   1¹/₃ cm × 1 cm

 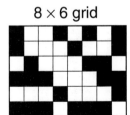

6 × 6 grid   8 × 6 grid

9 × 9 grid   12 × 9 grid

V V
H H

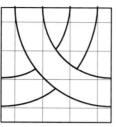 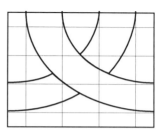

$3\ \text{cm} \times 3\ \text{cm}$ $\qquad\qquad$ $4\ \text{cm} \times 3\ \text{cm}$

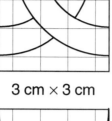 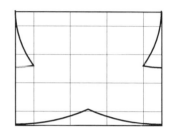

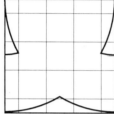 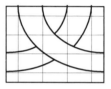

$2\ \text{cm} \times 2\ \text{cm}$ $\qquad$ $2\tfrac{2}{3}\ \text{cm} \times 2\ \text{cm}$

  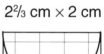

$1\,\text{cm} \times 1\,\text{cm}$ $\quad$ $1\tfrac{1}{3}\,\text{cm} \times 1\,\text{cm}$

 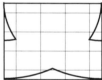 

6×6 grid $\qquad\qquad$ 8×6 grid

 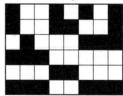

9×9 grid $\qquad\qquad$ 12×9 grid

140

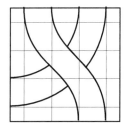 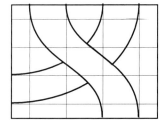

V V
H V

3 cm × 3 cm   4 cm × 3 cm

 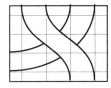

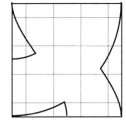

2 cm × 2 cm   2²⁄₃ cm × 2 cm

 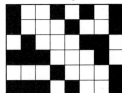

1 cm × 1 cm   1¹⁄₃ cm × 1 cm

6 × 6 grid   8 × 6 grid

9 × 9 grid   12 × 9 grid

V V
V D

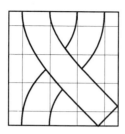 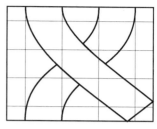

3 cm × 3 cm   4 cm × 3 cm

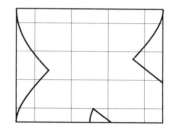

2 cm × 2 cm   2⅔ cm × 2 cm

 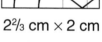

1 cm × 1 cm   1⅓ cm × 1 cm

 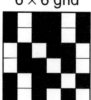

6 × 6 grid   8 × 6 grid

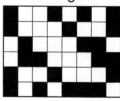

9 × 9 grid   12 × 9 grid

142

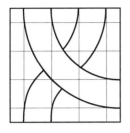 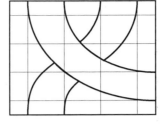

**V V
V H**

3 cm × 3 cm   4 cm × 3 cm

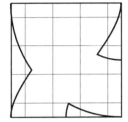 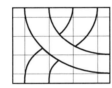

2 cm × 2 cm   2⅔ cm × 2 cm

1 cm × 1 cm   1⅓ cm × 1 cm

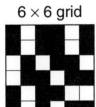 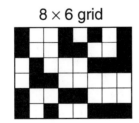

6 × 6 grid   8 × 6 grid

9 × 9 grid   12 × 9 grid

143

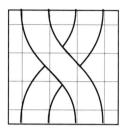 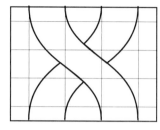

$3 \text{ cm} \times 3 \text{ cm}$ $4 \text{ cm} \times 3 \text{ cm}$

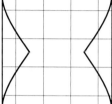 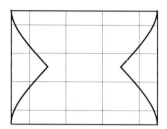

     $2 \text{ cm} \times 2 \text{ cm}$ $2\frac{2}{3} \text{ cm} \times 2 \text{ cm}$

$1 \text{cm} \times 1 \text{cm}$ $1\frac{1}{3} \text{cm} \times 1 \text{cm}$

   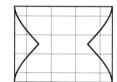

6×6 grid 8×6 grid

 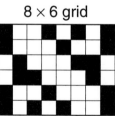

9×9 grid 12×9 grid

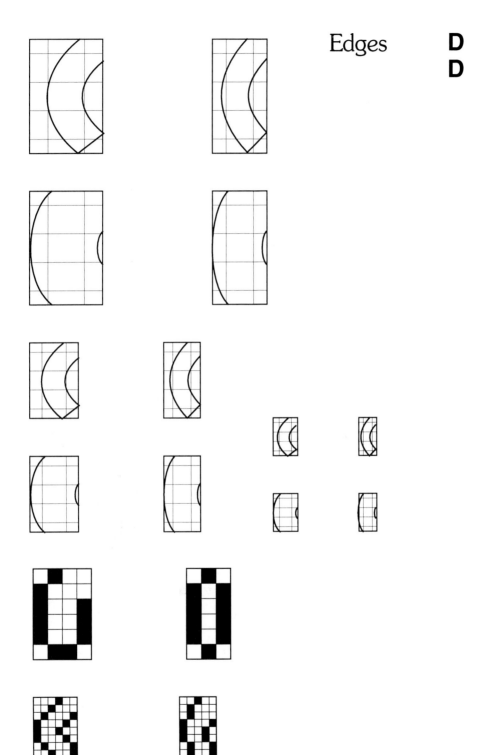

Edges

D
D

D
D

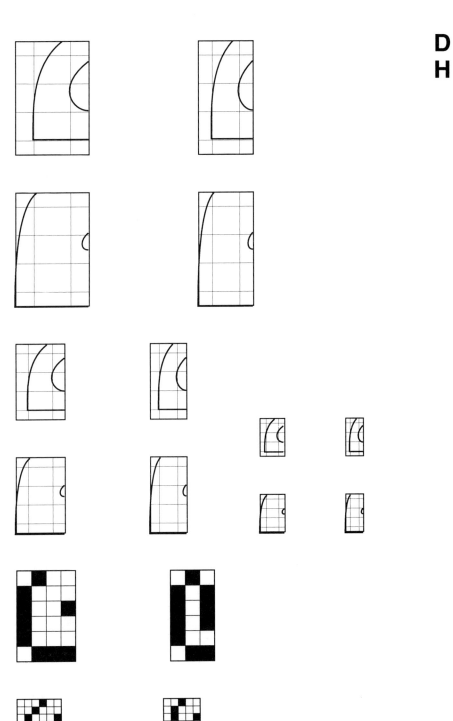

D

H

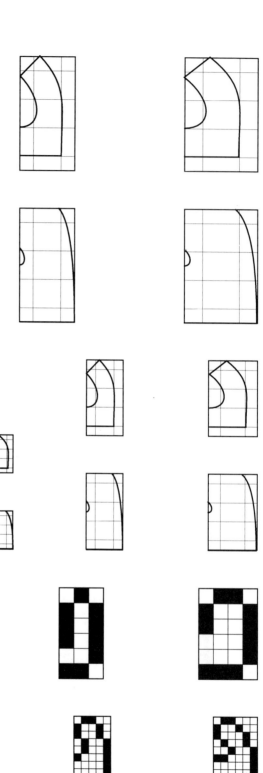

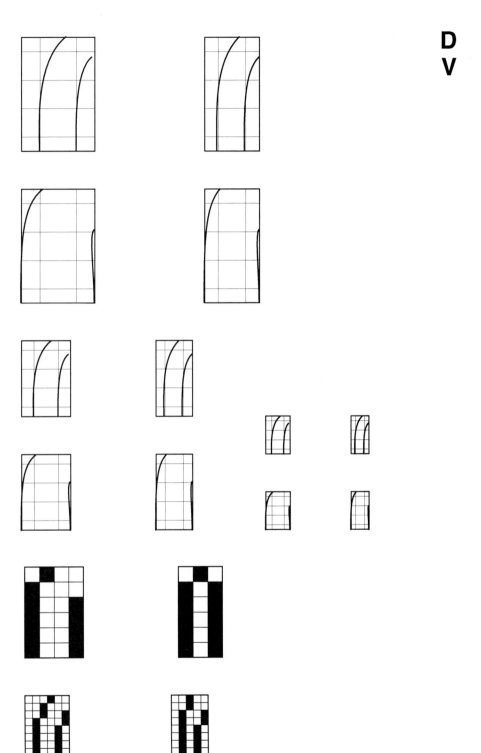

D
V

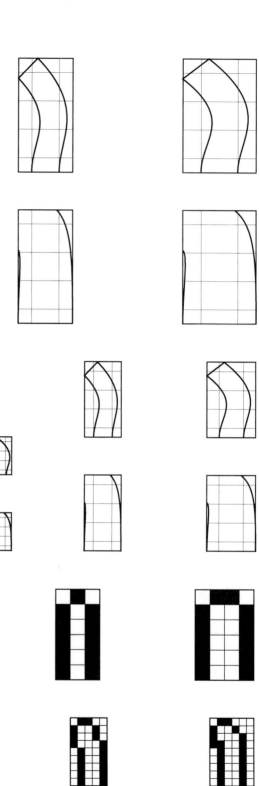

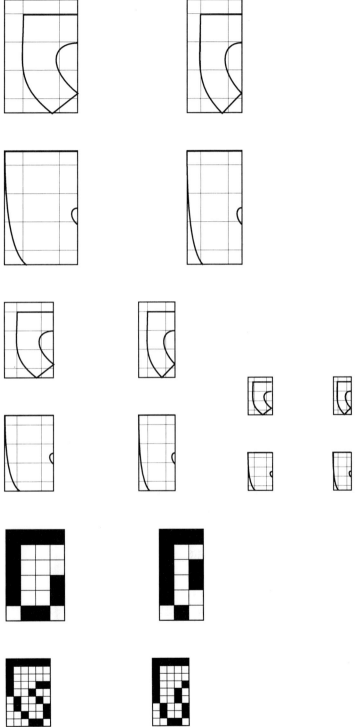

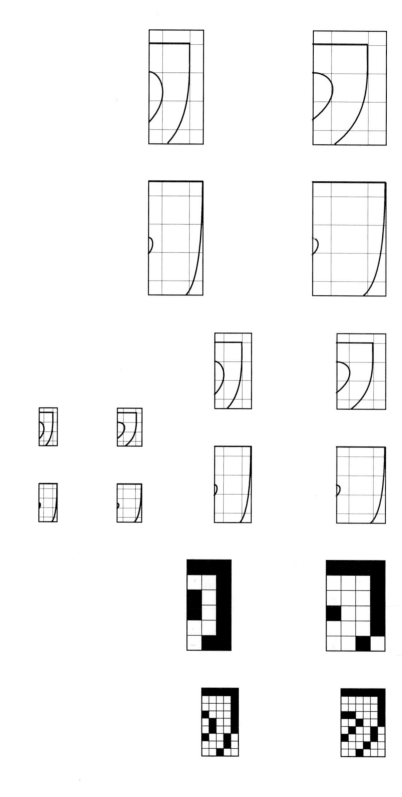

152

H
H

153

H
H

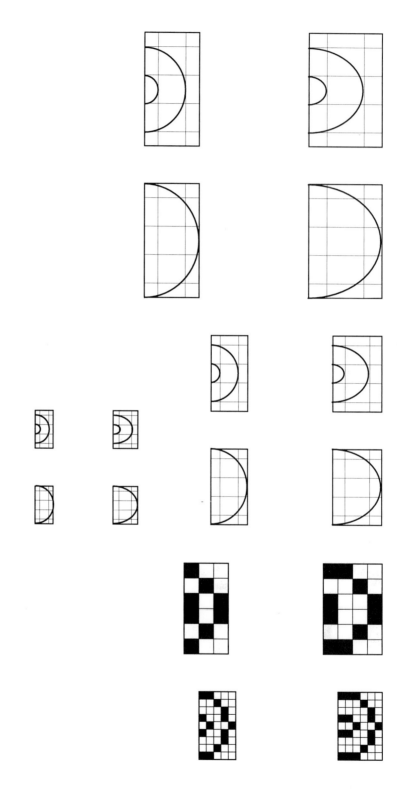

154

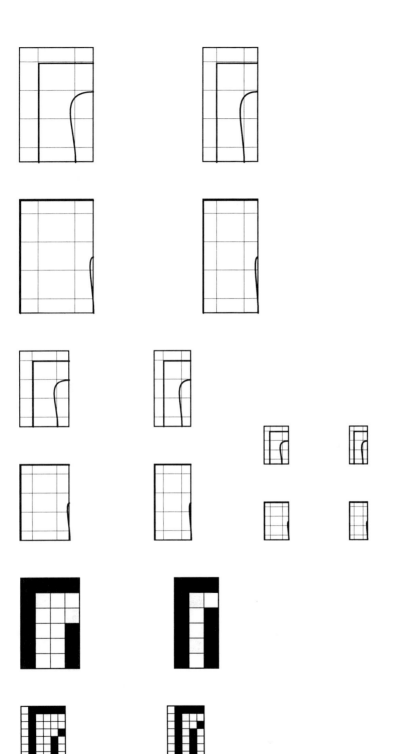

H
V

155

H
V

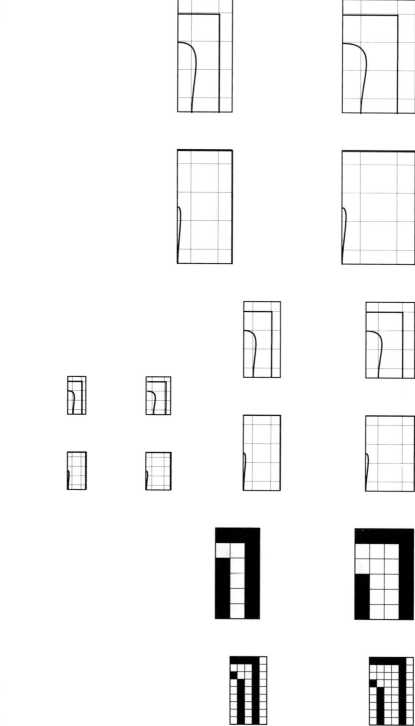

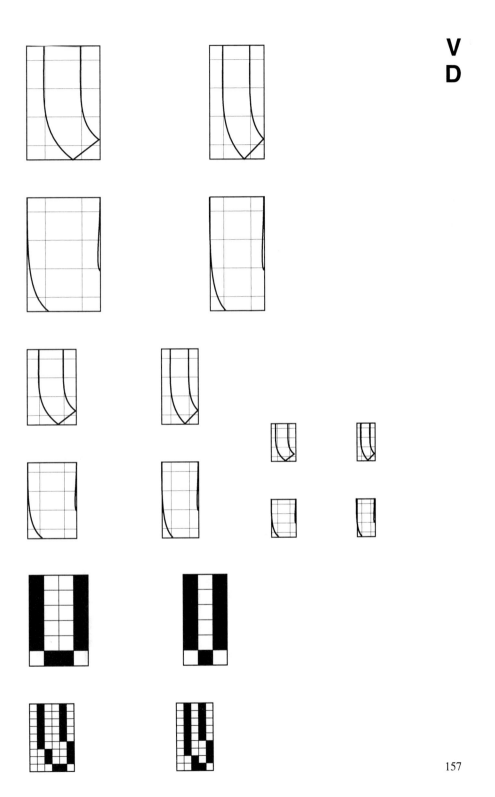

V
D

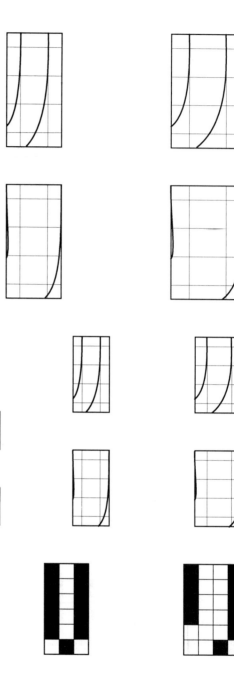

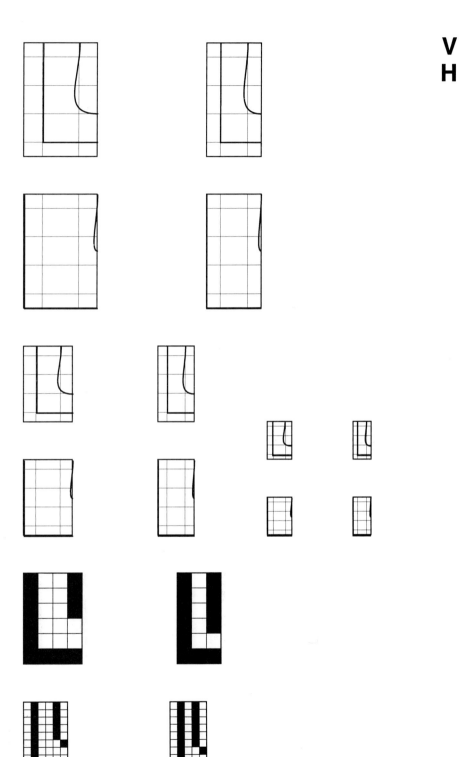

V
H

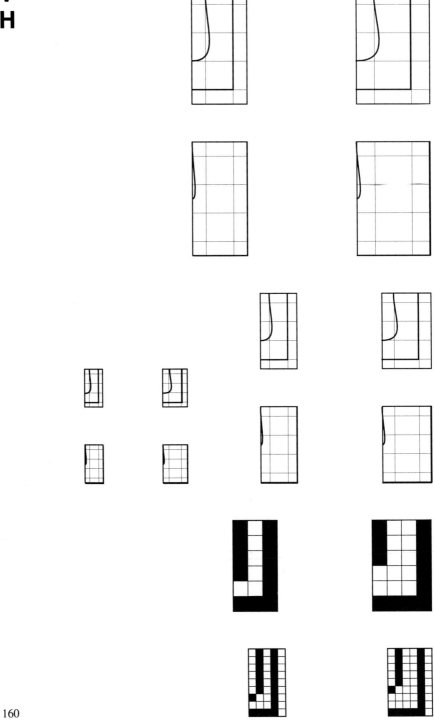

160

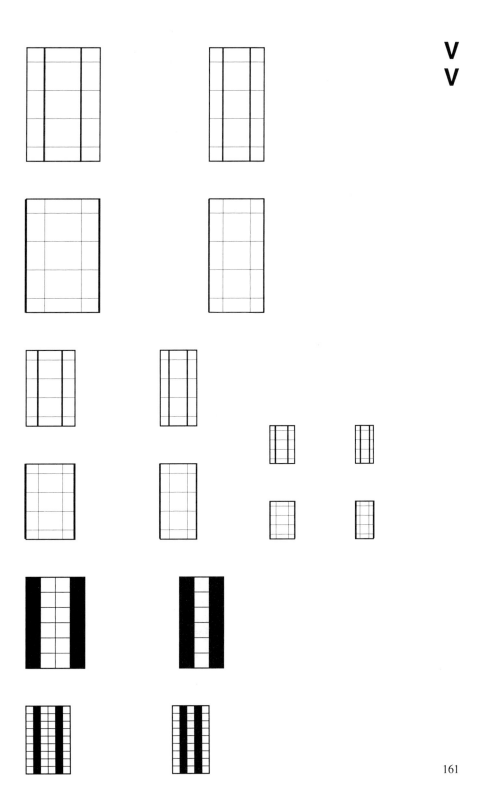

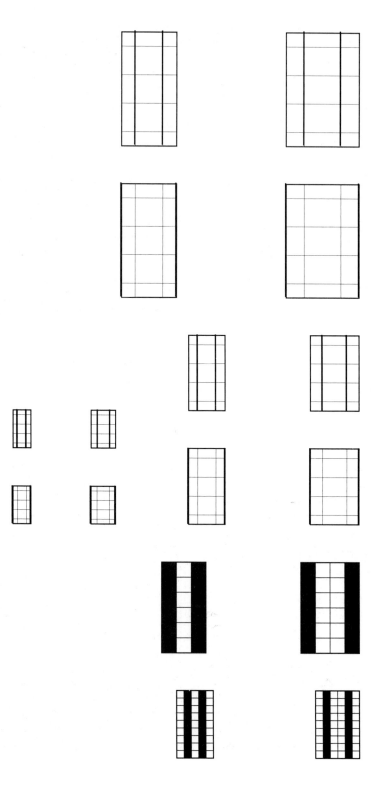

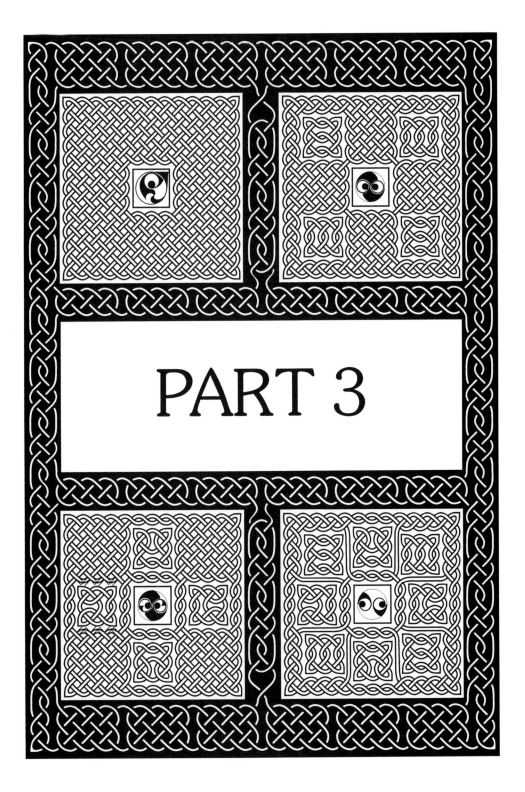

PART 3

Sourcebook

2 x 2
BORDER KNOTS

Total number of possible variations: 729

2 x 2
CLOSED KNOTS

Total number of possible variations: 81

2 x 3
BORDER KNOTS

Total number of possible
variations:
59,049

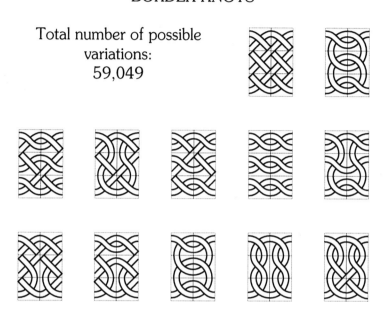

2 x 3
CLOSED KNOTS
Total number of possible variations: 2,187

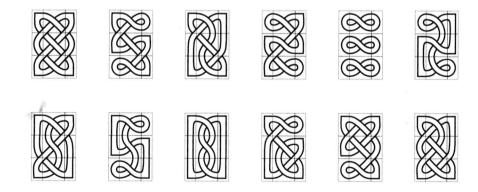

3 x 2
BORDER KNOTS

Total number of possible
variations:
19,683

3 x 2
CLOSED KNOTS

Total number of possible
variations:
2,187

3 x 3
BORDER KNOTS
Total number of possible variations:
14,348,907

3 x 3
CLOSED KNOTS
Total number of possible variations: 531,441

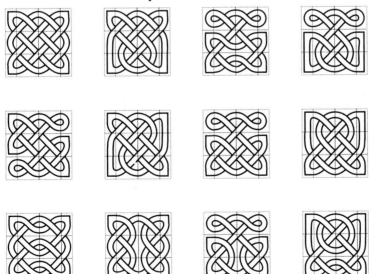

4 x 3
BORDER KNOTS
Total number of possible variations: 3,486,784,401

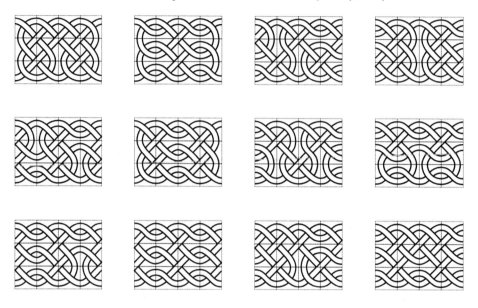

4 x 3
CLOSED KNOTS
Total number of possible variations: 129,140,163

3 x 4
BORDER KNOTS
Total number of possible variations: 10,460,353,203

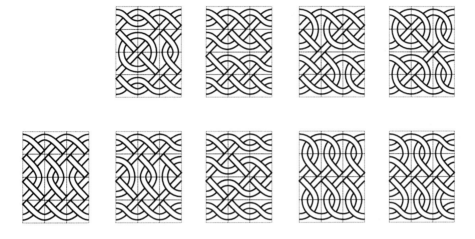

3 x 4
CLOSED KNOTS
Total number of possible variations: 129,140,163

4 x 4
BORDER KNOTS
Total number of possible variations: 22,876,792,454,961

4 x 4
CLOSED KNOTS
Total number of possible variations: 282,429,536,481

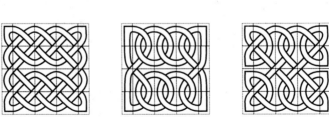

170

3 x 5
BORDER KNOTS
Total number of possible variations: 68,630,377,364,883

3 x 5
CLOSED KNOTS
Total number of possible variations: 31,381,059,609

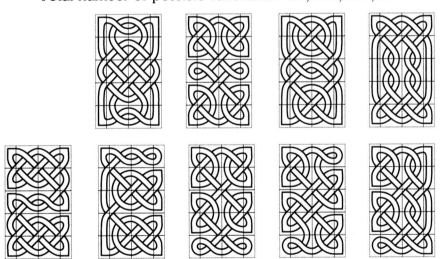

and so on and so forth, getting increasingly astronomical with every added grid line (as if 68 trillion (American style) was not enough!), but this should give you an idea of how easy it is to create new knots.

Variations on a theme

The following pages all contain knotwork that has had freehand treatments done to the original designs. Change a diagonal into a horizontal section, or into a vertical section...

or double up the knot and put together the variations...

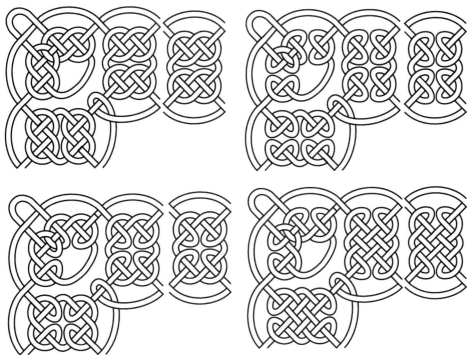

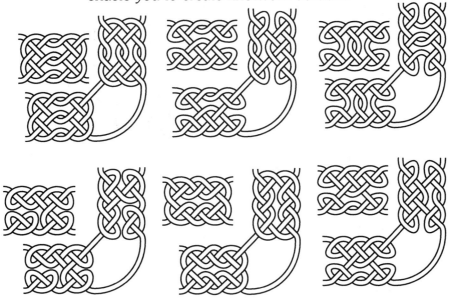

Or change the straight lines at top and bottom to curves.
All the knots on this page are shown with rotatable corner pieces to
enable you to create knotwork borders.

More variations

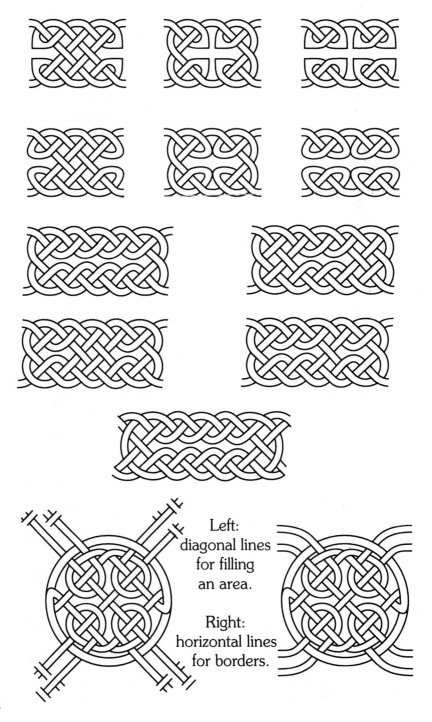

Left:
diagonal lines
for filling
an area.

Right:
horizontal lines
for borders.

174

More border knots and corners

Quarter circle –
rotate to complete

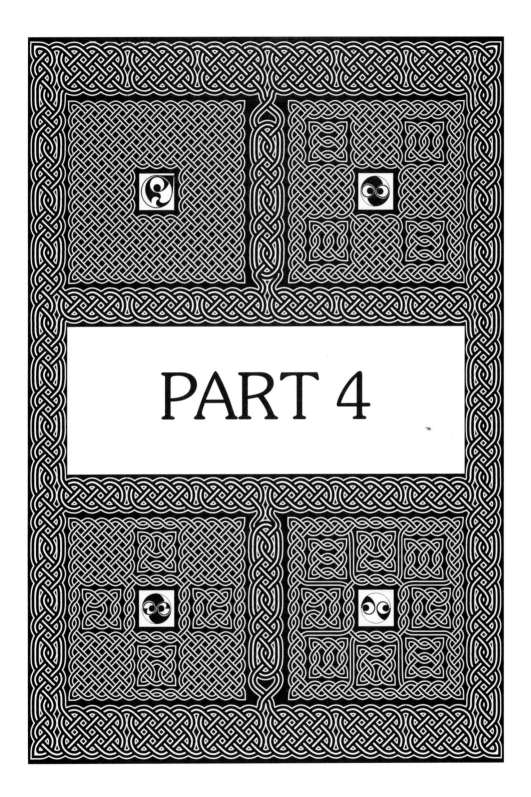

PART 4

Appendix 1 The sections
Diagonal sections

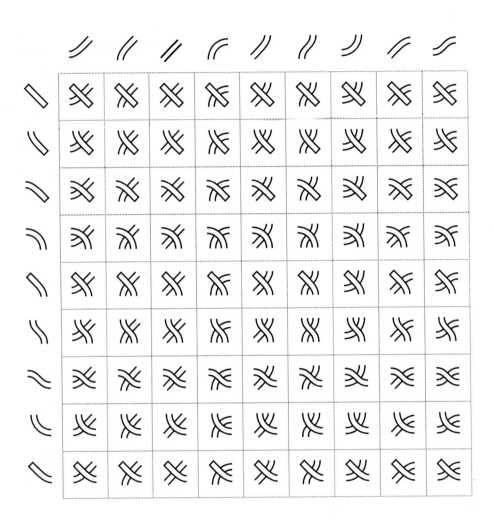

Horizontal sections

Vertical sections

Edge sections

Left-hand **Right-hand**

Appendix 2 Grids
45° semicircle grid

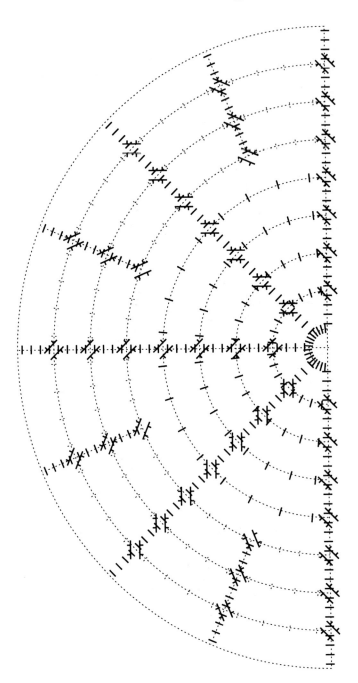

30° semicircle grid

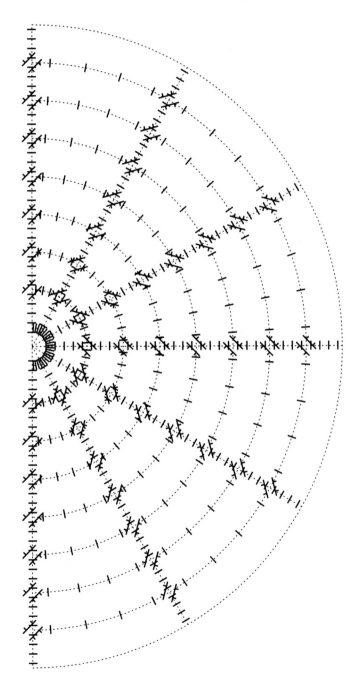

0.5 cm by 0.5 cm

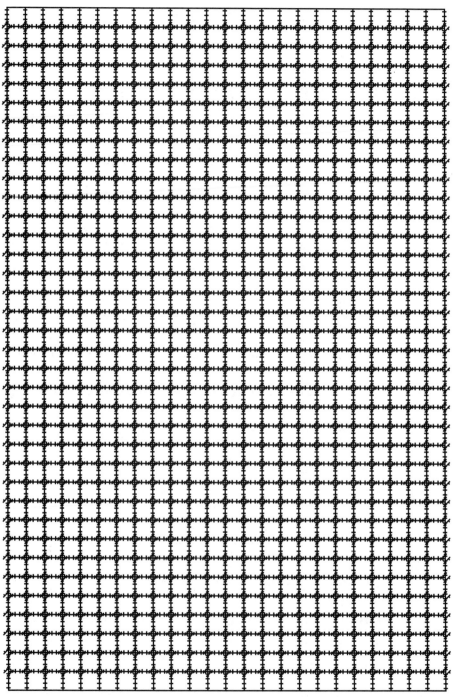

1 cm by 1 cm

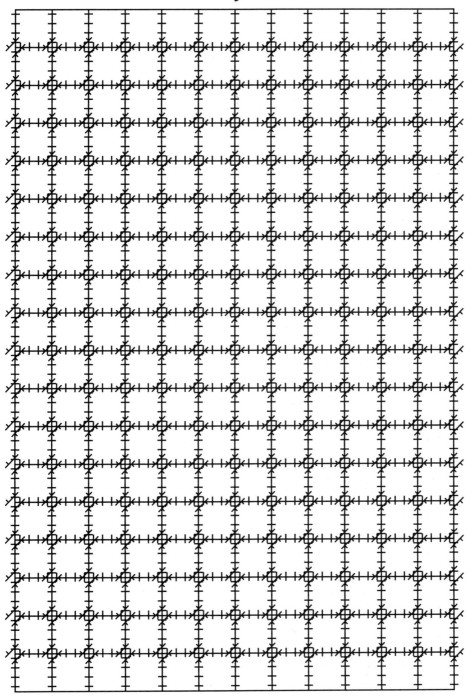

2 cm by 2 cm

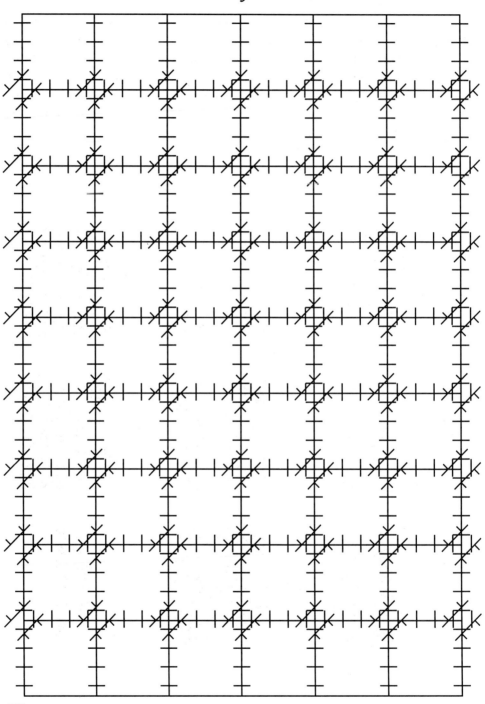

Appendix 3 Writing with knots

Using this method it is possible to write with knotwork. The letters are made up in much the same way as the letters on a digital display, using the vertical and horizontal gaps to make up the letters. The lettershapes, like digital displays, are very basic, but if you were to make the knots larger, or the sections smaller, you could design your own letters, which could look much smoother. Here is one of the most basic alphabets, which creates fairly readable text.

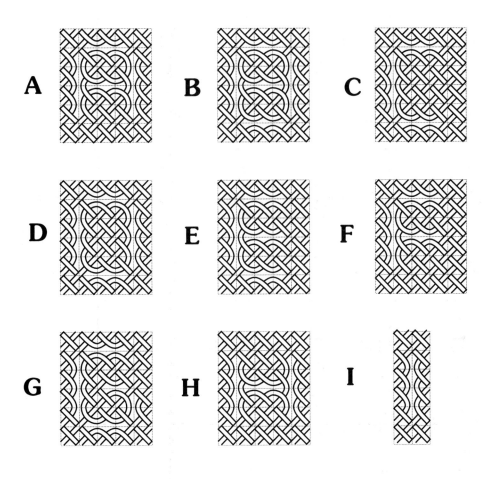

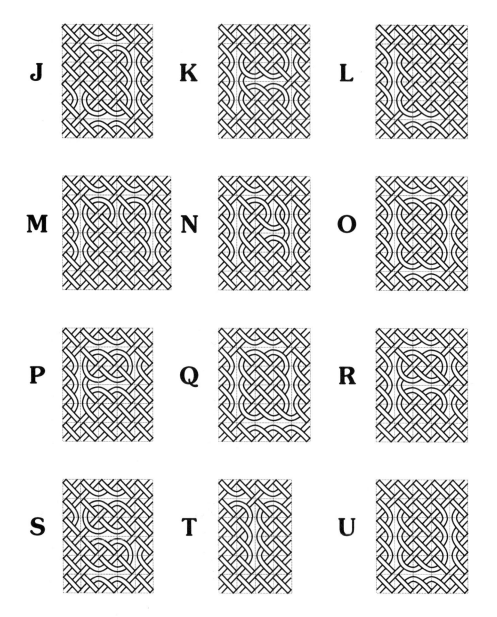

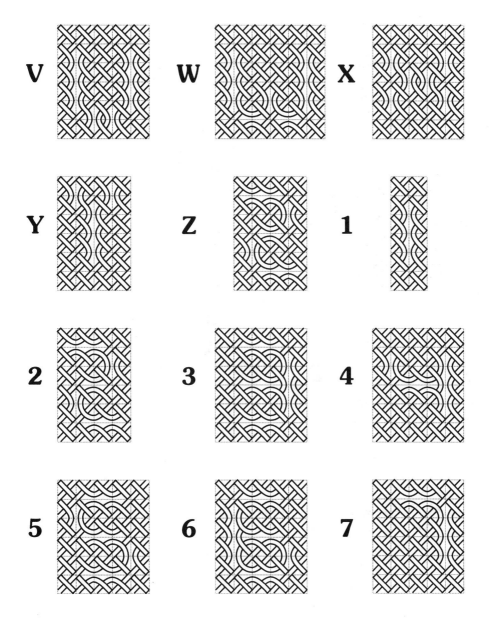

V

W

X

Y

Z

1

2

3

4

5

6

7

8  **9** **0**

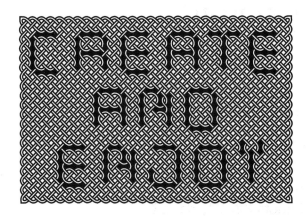

Index

Created as a companion to this book, ProScribe is a suite of elements which combine to create a fully comprehensive method of producing Celtic knotwork and designs on computer.

Years of research have gone into the creation of historically accurate designs and typefaces, all reproduced to the smallest detail.

ProScribe contains:

- 12 fonts based on the method in this book, producing an infinite variety of Celtic knotwork in four different styles

- 3 fonts for producing six different key patterns, each in 32 different styles

- 5 historically accurate typefaces to merge seamlessly with the knotwork designs (uncials, half-uncials and rustic capitals)

- 2 alphabets of illuminated capitals

- a large collection of scalable (eps format) historically accurate designs (spirals, animals, plants, borders, circular knotwork)

- an easy-to-use program which creates any complexity of design using the knotwork and key pattern fonts, for ready insertion into your word-processor or graphics program

- a history of Celtic designs, manuscripts and traditions

All fonts are supplied in Postscript® and TrueType® format. ProScribe is available for the Apple® Macintosh™ and IBM® compatible PC.

PreScribe, a special 'taster' of the ProScribe package, is available, containing samples of some of the fonts and artwork. PreScribe costs just £5, which is refundable against full purchase of ProScribe.

Please write for further information on ProScribe and/or a copy of PreScribe (cheques etc. payable to Crazy Diamond Designs).

C.D.D., The Crofts, Market Place, Abbots Bromley, Nr. Rugeley, Staffs., WS15 3BS, UK